Wishing you all th
discovering your

Vijay

Unknown Truth of Life

A guide to awaken creativity and intelligence

VIJAY PABBATHI

AuthorHouse™ UK Ltd.
500 Avebury Boulevard
Central Milton Keynes, MK9 2BE
www.authorhouse.co.uk
Phone: 08001974150

© 2009 Vijay Pabbathi. All Rights Reserved.

No part of this book may be reproduced, stored in a retrieval system, or transmitted by any means without the written permission of the author.

First published by AuthorHouse 2/16/2009

ISBN: 978-1-4389-4443-2 (sc)
ISBN: 978-1-4389-4444-9 (e)

Printed in the United States of America
Bloomington, Indiana

This book is printed on acid-free paper.

Acknowledgements

My understanding of Nature's Intelligence and how the human mind misleads us about the facts of life affairs has deepened considerably, particularly when I listened to Jiddu Krishnamurthy (a spiritual teacher who lived from 1895 to 1986). For this, I am indebted to him. My spontaneous understanding of Krishnamurthy's teachings is based on similar conclusions that I reached from my own understanding of nature.

I am profoundly grateful to Chuang Tzu and Lao Tzu for opening my eyes to many aspects of how 'Nature's Intelligence' functions. Both these teachers are great figures of early Taoist thought.

I am also deeply stimulated by the works of Fritjof Capra. Particularly, I am captured by his understanding about the interconnections and interdependencies between scientific concepts. I drew on both his earlier work *'Tao of Physics'*, and his later works including *'Turning point'* and *'The Hidden Connections'*. His conceptual frameworks are valuable resources and go beyond intellectual affairs to understand life intelligently. Professor Capra's work prompted me to understand that it is extremely important for all of us to translate scientific information for non-technical readers, so that by assembling coherent information from various fields, we will have a better chance of dealing with life intelligently and successfully. My insights, which are part of my personal development and my understanding about nature and ways of life, are presented in this book.

To Jean Gerard Sathish, my dear friend, whose debates helped me to verify my insights; I am deeply grateful to Sathish for listening and questioning my understanding. I also wish to express my deep gratitude to Rohini Sathish for listening to my insights and exploring the benefits of these insights in her own life situations.

I express appreciation to my friends Bala Rajasekharuni and CVL Srinivas for unconditional support and encouragement throughout the preparation of this book. Discussions with Bala prompted me to teach my insights to others.

I am obliged to Krishan Ramyead for many critical comments. In my journey toward understanding life, I have had many opportunities to discuss my insights with Krishan Ramyead. His questions have also helped me to improve the clarity of certain insights presented in this book.

To Alf Turner, for your inspirational discussions and philosophical questions. I deeply value our relationship. I also extend my gratitude to Grant Redstone and Joseph Cimino for informative discussions and support during the early stages of preparation of this book.

I am deeply grateful to Marliese Symons for her support, philosophical discussions, and valuable advice on numerous occasions. Her debates also helped me shape my insights into a presentable form. All of your discussions, Marliese, and your responses to my teachings have helped me to better understand life.

I am indebted to Nelson Monteiro for debates, fascinating conversations, and encouragement. His discussions helped me shape my thoughts into a presentable form.

I also express gratitude to Harsha Kantamneni and Vamsi Mohan Koka for encouragement and advice whenever I needed it.

To my students and friends who attended my seminars: I have learned much from you and acknowledge you for your participation in my journey toward understanding life.

I am grateful to Olwyn Hocking for her help in proofreading this manuscript and forming the final version of this book. I also thank **AuthorHouse's staff for helping me through the publication journey.**

Contents

Acknowledgements..1

1. Preface..7

2. Introduction..11

3. Wholeness of Life..17

4. Awakening Creativity...39

5. Living in Your Own Life..61

6. Being Intelligent..75

7. The Ultimate Purpose of Life 97

8. The Certainty of Life..125

9. The Absolute Truth 143

10. Summary..165

1. Preface

This book is intended for the general reader. However, I particularly think that it will be useful to young people who are interested in understanding life, and also to those people who wish to explore their natural gifts.

My recommendations are based on my personal experiences and are not based on intellectual propositions. If you are keen to understand life, you may need to test these insights within your own life experiences rather than merely depending on logical conclusions. I want you to rely on your own experimental results.

Understanding life does not require you to get a certificate or expertise. A need to acquire certificates makes you ignore a truer understanding of life. This is because when there is a need to be an expert in a particular field, the mind ignores facts that do not support one's aim. A deep passion to understand how to deal with our lives intelligently, and not because we want certificates in exchange for our understanding, helps us become better human beings. If we do not understand what we are doing and verify whether our strategies can further help us to survive, we are in danger of becoming extinct before nature makes a decision on the entire human race.

I have neither attempted to give the reader what he wants, nor attempted to give what I want. I wish to tell the reader what I see as facts and awaken the intelligence that he already has. In this book, we will go through a journey in which none of us are greater than one another. Thus we will destroy psychological barriers to uncover a cognitive skill that helps us to see the facts. In this journey, we will see the facts, although society does not necessarily respect them. Unless we have time and a deep interest in looking at the facts of life that exist beyond a value-based system, we will not possibility understand life as it is.

In this journey we will not consider opinions, because the facts do not require the support of opinions. We will park our opinions like we park our cars and walk away on a bumpy road, even if we do not like it – because this is what we must do if our interest is finding the unknown truth of life.

Whatever I describe is what I see as truth. It is not my focus to destroy or undermine any religion or established system of practice. Some of my statements in this book may appear to be anti-system, or anti-school, or anti-religion. My concern and interest lies beyond being anti-religion. It is not my fight to be anti-system. My point is that we should use whatever teachings are useful and move on with living in our own life. Once we let the system become more important, our life is compromised.

My concern is to explore what is it that makes man intelligent? Is it a system of practice or method? Or, it is seeing the mentality that is desperate for a system? Along those lines, I have used the examples of Buddha, although the insights are generally applicable to other systems of practice. My interest is our personal lives. My debates are about the mentality of minds that are following the systems; they are not about the teachers or systems themselves.

When I mention body mechanisms, I have mostly used non-technical terms. However, if the reader needs to see the technical information, he can find it in any medical textbook. I have not attempted to quote any reference because the nature of the information is really basic and can be found in any general medical textbook.

Please note that the approach to life recommended in this book is of value for both men and women. The word 'he', rather than 'he/she', is used generically, and this is for ease of reading.

If you wish to communicate with Author, his email address is as follows: vijay_p22@yahoo.co.uk

*   *   *

2. Introduction

There has been a remarkable development in man's intellect (thinking process) and the ways with which the intellect has been used in the development of science and technology. However, is an intellect that can deal efficiently with science and technology also capable of dealing with life affairs efficiently?

Man has accomplished tremendous technological advancements during the past 150 years. As far as outward achievements are concerned, man's progress is outstanding to date. However, the way that man deals with life has not been changed for centuries. It appears to me that there is no psychological maturity in man's thinking or how he handles life affairs. Whatever man has achieved to date is a fraction of what he is capable of accomplishing. In other words, many individuals are ignoring what they are naturally capable of doing in life. Man is striving to accomplish what he wants at the cost of losing some important psychological skills, such as recognising the facts in everyday life situations. Most of us are satisfied with merely fitting in with the social pattern. What is it that we need to understand in order to deal with life intelligently?

We think we are very logical people based on the scientific progress that we have made. Is being logical in our dealings with life sufficient for us to be intelligent in dealing with life situations and people? Is there really anything that science and logic cannot measure that gives you tangible answers to shape your life? It is important to enquire into these points so that our understanding can remain strong and coherent irrespective of where we find ourselves – in different cultures, different places around the world, and different times in the history of the human race.

Because man's intellect has proven very useful, we have an overemphasis on improving the efficiency of the intellect and aiming high to achieve certain end results. By pushing ourselves to achieve 'what we should become,' it is important to investigate whether we are losing important cognitive skills that are required to handle life efficiently.

Can the mind become intelligent and express creative natural abilities by achieving 'what we should become'? By making an effort to reach one of the top positions in society or struggling to meet psychological demands, can man express his creativity?

What is happening in society is that an overemphasis on sharpening the intellect is making many young people lose their original talents. Sharpening the intellect or striving to be an expert in a field may be useful to fit into society, but does that help an individual find a meaningful life? Does that help individuals discover their ultimate potential in life?

Many individuals are not expressing their innate gifts and abilities and are losing their original talents while under the impression that they are achieving their projected goals or dreams. Are your dreams or goals drawing on those natural talents with which you were born?

The insights presented in this book help dissolve the intrinsic barriers in our thinking and reveal certain natural secrets that help to deal with life affairs intelligently and creatively. These insights also reveal what we unconsciously miss out on in exchange for accomplishing something that can be applauded by society.

* * *

Natural laws are unchanging

Many natural examples that are particularly related to the human body are considered here to explain these insights. Such examples provide clues about nature's intelligence. Natural laws do not change from place to place or from time to time and are as dependable as gravitational force. Man may change flags, dress codes, languages, accents, foods, gods/goddesses, gospels, education, and culture, but nature's operations are beyond the capabilities of human mind to understand them, and outside of the scope of everything that man controls.

The human mind devises many plans to handle everyday life affairs, and man's strategies for making decisions about life are available from a variety of sources, including cultural beliefs, sacred texts, and modern psychology. However, the validity of these strategies depends on geographical area, time, and cultural or ethnic background. What is reliable in the West might be unreliable in the East. The more we follow man-made strategies, the more confusion emerges, as none of mankind's approaches are universal. Since natural laws are unchanging, it is useful to understand whether we can apply these laws to our lives. However, the strategies that nature has been following for billions of years do not change due to external values like power, money, and fame.

Natural secrets are rooted in the ways that nature functions to sustain health and life. I apply natural laws to everyday life situations, as presented in the following chapters. My reference point to correlate Nature's intelligence is the human body.

* * *

The human body as an example

The human body uses natural laws to achieve everything needed to maintain its health. These laws are simple and subject to experimentation. They are non-mystic, non-occult, and can be understood by non-technical audiences. Irrespective of the observer, these laws are involuntary, and independent of geographical area or time. Nature's 'intelligence' is an integral part of our bodies, our behaviour, and our everyday interactions with others.

For example, blood has to supply oxygen to all of the body's parts, whether it flows in the body of pauper or a prince. The lungs need to expand and collapse to keep you alive whether you are Japanese or British – or whether you speak English or Chinese. Nature does not change its rules even if you have a billion dollars in your bank account. Similarly, the functions of your body remain the same irrespective of your cultural background.

Man-made rules change according to requirements, but your heart has to beat and pump the blood to your body parts whether you are Christian, Hindu, or Jewish. Your body functions in the same way whether you feel chosen or not chosen. You may add titles or degrees to your name; you may think differently depending on your cultural and educational background. However, the body does not change how it functions. The heart beats in the same way whether you have a long beard or a shaven head.

*   *   *

Natural Laws are applicable to life affairs

In the human body, the functions of all its systems are interdependent and mutually supportive. All body parts develop initially from a single cell (a single energy), which is technically referred to as a zygote. Since all of the organs are products of a single energy, serving each other is simply serving the same intelligence. Thus, in both health and sickness, the individual organs are interconnected with all other parts or systems of the body. They have a symbiotic relationship in which no one organ or system is greater than the other. This network of relationships is similar to the partnership relationships among entities in ecosystems and provides important clues to help us comprehend the whole universe.

In my understanding, Nature's intelligence in our body is the same as the intelligence that we see in the ecosystems, and it is the same intelligence that controls human behaviour in everyday affairs. It is also traditional knowledge in India, China, and Japan that understanding our own living body – part of Nature's intelligence – is the key to understanding life itself.

*   *   *

3. Wholeness of Life

The Insight

Life is a unitary process in which problems and opportunities are interconnected. It is only a matter of time before we see one or the other. Thus the individual events of life have no independent existence. Understanding that life is a unitary process helps us to deal with life affairs efficiently.

When the mind understands that life moves in a non-linear fashion, the mind naturally expects every event of life to be discontinuous. Such understanding dissolves fear about the outcome so that man deals with life intelligently.

In a nutshell

Understanding life goes beyond the scope of logical thinking if you are prepared to handle the opposite events during successes and failures.

Everywhere in the world, man's attitude is to accomplish 'linear progress', which means: man seeks success, followed by success, followed by success, and so on. Man appreciates this continuous success. This pattern of attitudes remains the same in all contexts of life, irrespective of an individual's cultural and academic background. For example, man desperately needs linear success in his career, business, and when seeking attention from others. Regardless of the scale of their accomplishments, people are desperate for progress in a linear fashion from their endeavours.

The major but invisible problem with the attitude of linear progress is that the mind becomes impermeable to facts that do not fit with linear progress. The 'mentality of linear progress' itself leads to the loss of certain cognitive skills that are important for dealing with life affairs intelligently. This is primarily because the intellect is always busy: either occupied with being successful upon tasting success, or else solving problems (or avoiding pain) during disappointments. While the whole mind is focussing on the short-term benefit to the individual, judging by the criteria of linear progress, man loses the intelligence that is required to deal with life efficiently.

Furthermore, the 'attitude of linear progress' will lead man to follow the crowd and whatever else brings applause. This is because the applause from society and the mentality of linear progress will act as driving forces for each other. When a man follows the crowd or is dependent upon peer pressure, how can he be creative or intelligent? Dependency on social applause creates an invisible trap that sabotages the life of the individual. The original trap is our own attitude towards life, which is seeking progress in a linear fashion instead of understanding life itself.

A man who conceives a goal, within the mindset of linear progress, will inevitably feel fear about the end results. Thus, fear begins as soon as the goal begins.

> The approach of accomplishing linear progress itself engenders both uncertainty and fear about the end results.

Can we conceive goals without having fear about the end results, so that we can improve our productivity and personal efficiency? Can we structure our goals in a way that harmonises our actions with Nature's Intelligence? Can we teach our children a better strategy so that our children do not need to suffer fears whenever they pursue their goals?

Any attitude that breeds fear makes man stupid. As long as your mentality is based on linear progress, it really does not matter which religion or which God you follow; you will not be able to solve life's problems intelligently. The focus on linear progress unconsciously breeds troubles in every walk of life. Until you realise this fact, no saviour, guru, or scripture can help you. My emphasis is on your mentality, and not on gods or religions.

Since our happiness depends upon accomplishing progress in a linear fashion, we face disappointments whenever we have adverse circumstances because our attitude does not fit with what is presented by nature. Life events are unpredictable, and sometimes these events do not depend on man's efficiency.

I see this 'attitude of linear progress' as a trap in human thinking. If you are struggling to maintain your progress in a linear fashion, it makes no difference to your life whether you are spiritual or scientific. If you wish to accomplish progress in a linear fashion, the eyes see what they want to see and the ears listen to what they want to hear. Thus, the whole mind selectively perceives information in a way that supports your goals. Since the mind unconsciously avoids the facts, the uncertainty is built into every action.

> Everything in nature, except human thinking, follows the pattern of non-linearity. Every situation or process in nature is discontinuous, except man's thinking.

Whatever drives man to function in a linear fashion or to maintain continuity will ultimately destroy him. The search or effort to maintain continuity makes man unintelligent because looking for continuity is an idea that is not based in fact. The idea of continuity keeps man in an unnatural state of affairs. How do we solve this problem?

It really does not matter what strategy you apply to fix your problems unless we understand that our mentality is simultaneously breeding our problems in life. The situation is like a man who is unloading water from a boat that has a large hole. As long as you travel in such a boat, which has a large hole in the bottom, does it matter whether you are a Christian, Hindu, or Buddhist? The problem belongs to everyone and we all need to understand the situation – but not through theories, explanations, or philosophies.

How can we solve this problem? What enables the mind to see the facts of a situation? What enables man to see the wholeness of life when it does not flow in a linear fashion? How can man spontaneously become intelligent in dealing with this kind of problem?

The expectation of linear progress is also the approach that man applies to machines. As long as energy is supplied, the machine produces results in a linear fashion until it breaks down. Unfortunately, man applies the same approach that he applies to machines to dealing with life affairs. Does life work in a linear fashion? Can we deal with life intelligently using the kind of thinking that we apply to machines?

This chapter presents the insight that 'the events of life follow a wave-like motion (non-linear motion) in which the crests and troughs of the wave are comparable with favourable and adverse situations in everyday life affairs'. Furthermore, this insight is conveyed by natural examples and everyday life circumstances. Before explaining this insight, it is useful to look at the basic properties of the wave. Please skip the individual parts of this chapter if you are unfamiliar with scientific words.

* * *

Nature's way

Within the context of this chapter, understanding some basic features of wave motion will be useful for comprehending the insights I seek to present. A wave is an interrupted transfer of energy with a specific direction from a point of reference. The wave that we see on the sea surface is a typical representation of a wave that contains a crest (the highest point of the wave) and a trough (lowest point of the wave).

The propagation of energy with the alternating appearances of the crests and troughs is a typical feature of Nature's intelligence. The functional events (crests and troughs) of wave motion are inseparable, alternative, complementary, and dynamically interdependent. Excluding one – crest or trough – excludes the other.

The wave motion is one of the functional properties of the universe; this property can also be seen at a subatomic level. A species like man can come and go on the planet, but the wave motion is eternal. It exists with or without man.

In my understanding, the functional pattern of wave motion is conserved in nature. The pattern includes two functional units like crests and troughs. A similar pattern reveals itself in both biological and non-biological systems.

Examples of non-biological systems include: sound – the gap in musical notes – and the wave motion of electrons.

In biology, there are numerous examples available to understand this phenomenon. I will use the example of a beating heart. Understanding this helps us to correlate the intelligence of the body and life affairs.

The heart contracts to pump blood to supply oxygen to all of the body's parts. The heartbeat consists of contraction and relaxation, which are interdependent events. Loss of relaxation excludes the next contraction and vice versa. These events are alternative. Contraction requires the heart to relax before the onset of the next contraction and vice versa. These events gather momentum for each other and are mutually exclusive.

Both contraction and relaxation are complementary events within a single, functional reality – a heartbeat. Relaxation is equally important as contraction. The entire heartbeat disappears if one of these events interferes with the other. Man looks at these events as two different events for the purpose of understanding the heartbeat. In reality, both contraction and relaxation belong to a unity. Furthermore, both contraction and relaxation of the heart are spontaneous – which means that there is no time gap to think about their actions as these are not separate events.

Neither the event of contraction nor relaxation of the heart dominates the other. In fact, they cooperate with each other. The failure of these functions to cooperate with each other – or if one dominates the other – leads to disease. Thus, the relationship of contraction and relaxation is truly integrated. It appears that the purpose of contraction is to serve relaxation – and the purpose of relaxation is to allow the contraction.

Other biological examples include: the contraction and relaxation of muscles; pulse and interval of pulse; inhalation and exhalation within the breathing process; the emptying and refilling of glands to help secretion. Events like stimulation and inhibition of biological signals help in transferring important information to various cells and in the coordination of brain events.

*   *   *

Following the heart

Many people use the saying: *'I am following my heart'*. In the context of the presented insight, it appears to me that following the heart could be interpreted as approaching life with a non-linear attitude.

By following the heart, you will see that the disappointments in one area of life are connected to successes in a different part of life. One can see the connections of successes and failures as being like the contraction and relaxation of a beating heart.

If you are merely reacting to situations, such as when you are in trouble, your state of mind becomes impermeable to the facts of life affairs. Similarly, if you are unaware of the connections of life events like the contraction and relaxation of heart beating, your mind cannot deal with life affairs intelligently.

> If you are truly following your heart, you will expect that the successful phases of life are discontinuous – in the same way that the contractions of the heart are discontinuous.

Thus, you will not be surprised by the gaps in your successes. Similarly, you will also understand the connections between various life events. Thus, the attitude of non-linear progress, which is nothing but following your own heart, saves a lot of psychological energy.

Following your heart takes you to a psychological state in which the consequences of your actions become immaterial because your mind is prepared for the opposition when handling life. When the consequences are immaterial, fear disappears. As Jiddu Krishnamurthy (a spiritual teacher who lived from 1895 to 1986) suggested, the loss of fear makes the mind intelligent. Thus you will have a chance to improve your productivity and personal efficiency, as your actions will be devoid of fear from the outset.

The secret of a beating heart is directly applicable to everyday life circumstances in which the useful and useless events of life are functional events within our own evolution.

Understanding that 'life events function like a beating heart' helps us to see a different dimension of life that is different from the way that we have been encouraged to see it. For example, your partner may appear full of love one day, and another day she may appear to be angry. If you have already introduced a gap in your expectations, you will save tremendous psychological energy by not reacting to situations as they directly appear.

Such an understanding about the totality of life affairs reduces your reactions to situations so that clarity emerges. If you are seeking attention in a linear fashion, your attitude will inevitably push you to a neurotic psychological state in which disappointments will be unavoidable because nature does not work according to the desires of intellect.

If you love your partner using your mind, then your mind will expect a linear progress in your relationship. If you truly love your partner with your heart, then your actions and expectations will be discontinuous. Thus, an understanding of the way that your heart works can be applied to all other areas of life.

A scientist who desperately wishes to produce data in order to publish his results will resist true objective observation of the experiments. Because of the psychological urge to produce results from a perspective of linearity, the mind will be exposed to fear and resist the facts. On other hand, if discontinuity is accepted as the norm, the scientist will have a better chance of observing the facts more objectively without forcing his mind in an unnatural direction.

Unknown Truth of Life

Another example of this is that students concentrate on their studies in a linear fashion, based on academic pressure. If students introduce a gap between the periods of concentration, their learning process will be more efficient. See whether this works in your own experience.

* * *

The life as a whole

In my understanding, life is a unitary process in which problems and opportunities are interconnected with each other. It is only a matter of time before you see one or the other. What can make man appreciate this fact? Most of us never see the wholeness of life because we are concerned with meeting our own immediate psychological demands in times of both good and bad.

I would also like to emphasise that when life is seen as single unit, the mind will automatically look for the way in which each individual event influences other events. Such curiosity helps man to prepare to handle opposing events in life. For example, when you are in a successful phase, your mind tends to prepare for opposite events while you enjoy your success. When you are in trouble, your mind will automatically investigate which successes are connected to each of your disappointments.

> The psychological demand for continuous progress makes the mind impermeable to the facts of life.

The mind that is prepared to consider opposite events during success and failures spontaneously becomes intelligent. By incorporating the attitude of non-linear progress in daily endeavours, man can appreciate the hidden connections among the different areas of life. When a mind sees the hidden connections of life through the lens of its own personal experience, it will unconsciously become aware of the totality of life.

Problems and opportunities in life are variable according to each individual's life circumstances. Examples of life events are: passing an exam; a partner leaving; getting an ideal job; the illness of a family member; finding an ideal partner; humiliation at the workplace; giving birth to a baby; a financial breakthrough; victory in a lawsuit; success in sports. According to the insight presented, these various life events are interrelated, and one can understand life events better if one treats them as unitary processes.

The mind cannot appreciate life as a whole as long as it feels the need to accomplish progress in a linear fashion. The psychological demand for continuous progress makes the mind impermeable to the facts of life. A man who is desperate for linear progress is poised to ignore the present life in exchange for a hypothetical future. When life is

Unknown Truth of Life

ignored in this fashion, what he accomplishes has marginal value.

A mind that cannot appreciate non-linearity as an eternal pattern seeks a separate meaning for life and ignores life itself. As long as you are encouraged to succeed in a linear fashion, you will inevitably struggle, and have little chance to understand life as a whole. Your intellect will tend to argue about the evidence as long as you do not witness the facts based on your own life affairs. Of course, the intellect argues against this approach because understanding the hidden connections of life means that there will be less emphasis on the intellect. That is why intellectual propositions may not agree with this insight.

For example, if you miss a train, you will feel disappointed because you may want to attend an important business meeting. The frustration may become deeper if you cannot even find an alternative means of transport. There may be many hundreds of reasons why you could not catch that train. You may have been poised to meet your life partner who has also missed the same train. You might have saved yourself from an embarrassing business meeting by not attending the meeting in time. The way in which missing that train is linked to your life cannot be understood by the intellect from the outset. This is because your thinking is part of the life process. In other words, when the experimenter is part of the experiment, he cannot make a true observation. Therefore, it is natural for anyone to react to specific situations. However, a man who sees life as a whole will be deeply interested in seeing the invisible connections. Such a man will look out for unfolding opportunities instead of reacting to situations, such as when he misses the train.

If you are serious about understanding the true nature of human life and how various life events are interconnected, then the following exercise will help you.

> When you face a disappointment, instead of reacting to the situation, it is wise to observe how the disappointment is leading to a new situation or series of events that will ultimately result in your benefit.

Similarly, when you have success, try to see whether the successful events might lead to adverse situations in life. Since most people do not reveal those events that are not appreciated by society, it is difficult to obtain a true account of life events from others. Instead, you can understand your own life situations or analyse the situations of people who are close to you.

It is a misconception in society that the most educated people know more about life. In fact, the most educated people deal with fragments of life and try to fix each fragment separately. Expertise is useful for performing a surgical operation or piloting an aeroplane or administrating your business. I am not arguing against applying expertise when performing these external affairs. Expertise is different in regards to application to life events because dealing with life requires an understanding of the wholeness of life. An expert may be good at using a formula, but when it comes to dealing with life, he fails to understand life as a unitary process.

*   *   *

The hidden connections of life

Understanding life as a whole makes man intelligent so that one can see the hidden connections of life from the outset. If the mind sees individual events as whole, it will not merely react to individual situations; rather, it will respond directly through action as opposed to dealing with debates.

Like the crests and troughs of a wave, both successful events and disappointments are an integral part of the universe. Man becomes happy or unhappy depending on the presentation of situations or choices. A change in presentation in a given situation triggers emotional reactions (either happiness or anxiety, for example). This is why many people cannot see the link between different events of life.

For instance, sunny days are followed by rainy days and vice versa. If you do not want the rainy day, the sunny day also disappears. We cannot choose one without the other, since both events belong to the single energy. The generation of these events is not subject to the individual requirements, but is part of the natural balance of the universe. It is a futile effort to respond emotionally to a rainy day because rainy days set the stage for the sunny days.

The personal requirement of wanting a sunny day or a rainy day is subjective. As far as reality is concerned, sunny days have equal value to rainy days, as both units are part of the whole. Both rainy days and sunny days are one dynamic unit provided for by Nature's Intelligence. Let me provide some examples to help the reader further understand this concept.

Warren Edward Buffett (born in 1930, in Nebraska, USA) is a businessman and philanthropist. In 1950, Harvard University did not accept his application to join the business school. This led him to attend Columbia, and a series of life experiences further led him to become one of the world's greatest stock market investors. Thus the disappointment that he could not join Harvard was an integral part of his later success.

According to news reports, he announced in June of 2006 that he would be donating a large amount of money to charities. Thus, his early disappointments are further interconnected with his charitable donations.

Mahatma Gandhi (1869–1948, India) was insulted and ordered out of a train when he was travelling in South Africa in 1893 because of his colour. This experience and other later experiences with the British Government prepared him to lead India's fight for freedom and to remain as the one of the greatest leaders in the twentieth century. Thus,

Unknown Truth of Life

a personal humiliation in 1893 was connected to India's eventual freedom from British rule in 1947.

Nobel laureate Sir Alexander Fleming (born in Ayrshire, Scotland, 1881–1955) wanted to be a surgeon, but became a bacteriologist. His new career propelled him towards his discovery of penicillin. Had his plans to become a surgeon been successful, he would not have discovered penicillin. Furthermore, millions of lives would not have been saved during the Second World War without the aid of his discovery.

Fleming's disappointment in not becoming a surgeon is intertwined with his crowning success of receiving a Nobel Prize for his discovery of penicillin. It is clear that we sometimes feel upset when we do not accomplish what we are looking for, though we often do not even consider the idea that Nature forces us to access the best possible outcome that will help us as well as others.

Sometimes we cannot see the connections between ordinary events and a crowning achievement. We only appreciate such connections with hindsight. Edward Jenner (born in Gloucestershire, England, 1749–1823) was a country doctor who was fascinated at the age of nineteen by a rural tale that 'milkmaids who get the non-life-threatening form of cowpox will not get smallpox [a life-threatening disease] itself'.

Based on his exposure to his rural surroundings, Jenner developed his theory that the fluid in blisters is useful for protection from infection. The treatment he developed became very successful, saved many millions of people around the world, and led to many other scientific discoveries. My emphasis is that we cannot see the connections among the various events of our lives. Sometimes events that seem insignificant may prove to be the most useful.

Consider further the well-known story of Michael Benedum (born in West Virginia, USA). Benedum offered a seat on a train to a stranger (John Worthington) who was the general superintendent of the South Penn Oil Company. This chance encounter helped him to obtain a job in the company. Later in his life, he became one of the most successful oil and gas corporation leaders in the United States. An event such as offering a seat to stranger in a busy train changed his whole life.

> It is impossible to see the hidden connections of life based on logical thinking. This is because the logical thinking does not accept that life moves in non-linear fashion.

The point is that it is impossible to see the hidden connections in life by using academic logic. However, if we understand that life is a unitary process and individual events do not follow the sequences that fit with our academic equations, there is a possibility that we can understand life beyond the scope of logical conclusions.

Unknown Truth of Life

The example below illustrates a real-life example. All of these events are taken from the successive phases of the life of the same individual, and thus these events are natural.

One of my friends failed an exam during his school studies. Although he had a well-established record of his ability in scientific subjects, he was not accepted into medical school because of his low mark in a language test. The situation was extremely humiliating for his family at that point.

After a career break, he joined veterinary school, where he met his future wife. Had he passed all his exams during his attempt to enter medical school, he would not have met the lady of his choice. The situation that humiliated his family ultimately led to his marrying the right partner.

Soon after the wedding, he went through financial hardship. Despite his financial struggle, he finished his Ph.D. and became a scientist. After his scientific success, he then became ill and underwent a surgical operation in which his life was at risk. Fortunately, after a period of convalescence, he continued his successful professional career and then became a lecturer. Despite his successful career, he is currently going through some life problems.

The previous example shows how favourable and adverse events of life are intertwined. The best way to verify whether this insight is useful is to list all the good and bad events that have happened in your life and plot the events on a graph to verify whether your life follows the suggested pattern or any other pattern. For example, represent the positive events as crests and negative events as troughs, in chronological order. Use this to verify whether your life events follow a pattern.

You can also analyse the life events of other people provided that you have access to a true account of their life events. I emphasise also that the hidden connections of life events cannot be understood unless we treat all of our life events as a unity. All life events are interrelated and therefore must be understood together, as shown in the above example.

Life is inclusive

Fundamentally, logical thinking fulfils certain ends. Its function is based on self-interest, motive, incentives, and so forth. Everything that is handled by logical thinking involves end results and incentives. When we approach our lives using logical thinking (the intellect), we unconsciously look for incentive or profit in every action. Dealing with life affairs requires using unconscious abilities such as happiness, peace, love, humility, creativity, beauty, and compassion. These qualities are not part of logical thinking (intellect). This is why the intellectual definitions of happiness, peace, creativity, and love are different from the way that people experience these emotions. Intellect, by its nature, incorporates self-interest in everything that it plans.

Life is inclusive of everything that involves both intellect and unconscious qualities. When man does not struggle to accomplish progress in a linear fashion, he develops sensitivity to these unconscious qualities. Intellect alone may be enough to deal with a machine successfully. However, if one applies intellect alone to life without incorporating qualities like love, peace, creativity, and happiness, life is destroyed.

Life cannot be understood with reason (intellect) alone. It is possible, however, to understand life with a quiet mind that is not busy in meeting psychological demands. Man can solve his life problems efficiently and intelligently if he stops using exclusively logical thinking. If you try to apply logic to all of your pursuits, you will end up discovering something that provides incentive, as opposed to the truth of life situations. This is your decision.

* * *

Applications

1. I will not be able to handle life affairs intelligently as long as I feel fear in my actions. I, therefore, will investigate whether seeking progress in a linear fashion is detrimental in my endeavours.

2. I understand that if my mind is prepared to handle the opposite events during successes and failures, I will be able to handle my life intelligently. This awareness will vanquish my fear about the outcome of my endeavours and help me to be vigilant in the event of success.

3. I will explore whether the individual events of my life have connections to see whether the insight of the 'wholeness of life' will save me from wasting psychological energy.

* * *

4. Awakening Creativity

The Insight

The mind that is prepared to be anonymous conserves psychological energy and awakens creativity.

Everything in the universe follows the 'path of least resistance'. Creativity is the result of moving in the same direction as nature.

When you naturally respond to situations and people, you will find your true nature, which is the expression of the divinity that is inside you. Such a natural response, in which the mind does not project what it wants, will have access to creative insights.

In a nutshell

Anonymity is a precursor for creativity............ Detachment to logical thinking awakens creativity.

Because man's intellect has been very useful across the world, there is an overemphasis on improving the efficiency of the intellect and aiming high to achieve certain end results. When pushing ourselves to achieve 'what we should become', we need to investigate whether we are losing important skills that are required for us to handle life efficiently. Can the mind become intelligent and express creative natural abilities by achieving 'what we should become'? By making an effort to reach one of the top positions in society or struggling to meet psychological demands, can man express his creativity?

Many people wish to be distinguished and famous. A sense of superiority and self-importance are built into their actions. We generally do not see anyone who does not want glory or honour or pride. However, do these feelings help the human mind to be creative? Are these feeling of self-importance in any way limiting the capabilities of man and thus preventing the growth of consciousness? My inquiry is: what is the cost of having such feelings? Are we giving away our lives and extraordinary abilities in exchange for attributes like self-importance?

Man created a cultural and educational system in which everyone craves laurels, prizes, and distinctions. Being distinguished is respected in our society. The struggle to be distinguished makes people deprecate the present in exchange for uncertain future outcomes. Furthermore, the arduous tasks involved in the model of becoming distinguished consume the individual's psychological energy — which then blocks creative output.

When the future becomes too important, the mind operates from an achievement-oriented mindset in which happiness depends on being distinguished from other people. It creates a situation in which 'I can do something that no one else can do'. Thus a mind that is constantly involved in proving its superiority can never bring about universal brotherhood.

Our perception is based on external values like being distinguished for recognition, accomplishing family honour or glory, or feeling pride. If an entire group or population reaches the pinnacle of a skill, then one person cannot be regarded as outstanding. We appear to have an unconscious necessity for other people to not accomplish things with the same efficiency as we do. If everyone accomplishes tasks at the same level of efficiency, how can one person attain distinction? Is it not true that we push our children to accomplish something great compared to others, and therefore prepare them to suffer, based on our own sense of self-importance? Let us inquire into these points – if we maintain understanding and clarity throughout the inquiry, it will prompt the right action.

Creativity is a psychological state in which the mind brings novel information from nothingness or an unknown source. If the insights come from nothingness and not from training, any description that we give using the intellect is not going to be sufficient for describing absolutely pure creativity. That means that the creative mind evokes novel insights that are not based on the intellect. Intellectual thought may provide volumes of information about creativity. I am not talking about the intellectual proposition of creativity. Let us look at Nature's way.

*   *   *

Nature's way

Let us consider natural situations to deepen our inquiry. For this purpose, I need to use a natural example. In health, the human body is forgotten. I mean that a person is not conscious of their bodily functions when they are healthy. Nature's intelligence maintains anonymity in health. In every second, the body strives to maintain anonymity. For example, the body ensures that you are not conscious of your kidneys when they are healthy. If you think of your kidneys, you may need to see a doctor, as pain in the kidney can be felt only in disease. Maintaining anonymity is nothing but maintaining health.

In the human body, disease begins when the conscious distinction of individual functions begins. For example, your heart will distinguish itself if it beats faster and faster and cannot be controlled.

Everything (Nature's Intelligence) inside our bodies and outside our bodies functions in the same way, except our minds. Distinctions are very meaningful to the mind. Man always tries to be distinguished.

> Nature gives equal importance to everything, like the equal nourishment of every cell in the human body, for example. It is only the perception of the human mind that tries to distinguish itself and feel superior to others.

The whole idea of being outstanding exists only in the mind. Being anonymous is the property of Nature's Intelligence and thus nature decrees that every organ in the body be anonymous as an aspect of health. The paradigm that brings health to the body does not appeal to the human mind. If nature had followed man's way, the whole of evolution could have been terminated long before the evolution of man.

* * *

Precursor for creativity

It is an intellectual approach to be eminent or feel superior. Intellect is useful in so many ways, but can it be trained to be creative? Creativity is the result of using psychological space that does not belong to the intellect; it is an unconscious ability. All unconscious abilities that are not in man's control follow the rules of nature. Anonymity, or 'not trying to be distinguished', is one such attribute of nature. If something is eminent, nature uses such a signal as a process of disease. It is common knowledge that nature has endless creativity. How can man be creative while following rules that are in opposition to nature?

> Anonymity is a precursor for creativity. You will cross the boundaries of human thinking when you are prepared to be anonymous and bring creative output that the world has never seen before.

If man is not exposed to such psychological demands such as being famous or extraordinary person, and does not feel bad for being anonymous, then he sets a fertile ground for the growth of his consciousness. Having such a psychological state is to have the right tools for being creative. Actions that emerge from the psychological state of being anonymous lead you to evoke creativity. If we understand that our habits are excluding creativity, then there is a possibility that we will change our habits.

Every child is born with creative abilities. We tend to isolate their true nature by attempting to engender in them what interests us. By promoting self-interest, which outwardly appears as love, we thoughtlessly ignore the child's own innate creative abilities. The cost of keeping the parent's self-interest is the sacrifice the child's creative abilities.

Unless you set an example yourself, there is no possibility that a child can learn. Once children see your way of life and how you are influencing society, it is easy for them to learn based on your example. If you try to teach something without yourself being changed, it is the only matter of time before your teachings become moot.

When children use their psychological energy to generate creative output, they will help themselves and be blessings to the world. If you make them fit for competitive society, sooner or later they harm themselves either directly or indirectly. This is your decision.

Anonymity is a precursor for creativity – I see this as a fact. Creativity has to be invited by the mind based on our ways of life rather than by following intellectual methods. The intellect may be useful for translating one's creative efforts into academic language or formulae so that the world can understand your creative output, but the translator (the intellect) is not the creator.

Whether you wish to have creativity or self-importance is your decision. Whenever you make an effort to be a clever person or a great person, be aware of the cost of such inclinations.

* * *

Vijay Pabbathi

Going beyond the logical thinking

If you wish to depend exclusively upon on logical thinking, then logic or reason prevents creative output. As long as reason is used to interpret observations or creative insights or solutions, then we can use reason intelligently. Reason itself cannot enable man to discover creative solutions, however.

The mind is a collective process of thinking in which memory, learning, understanding, and reasoning are involved. The human mind has accomplished a number of successes, including technological, scientific, and medical achievements. Because our minds are able to invent many scientific tools and have been very helpful in technological advancement, we may think that we have achieved a lot. However, my perception is that what we have accomplished to date is a fraction of what is possible for us to accomplish. This appears to me to be a fact because our approach to life is intellectual. It appears to me that the unconscious abilities like creativity are excluded if we are not able to go beyond the use of intellect.

As long as the mind uses logic, the mind perceives that everything is going all right. This is primarily because thinking logically employs more neural pathways and more functional capability from brain tissue. Whenever we do not generate logical ideas, the mind regards spontaneous insights as insane, as it cannot find logic to justify these thoughts. Therefore, the adherence to logic is an adherence to its functional involvement in a given task, and the rejection of ideas has nothing to do with reality.

People who work in creative fields are often fulfilled because their nature of work does not depend on logical conclusions. Creativity happens to individuals when they express their innate abilities and go beyond what they have learned. The nature of creativity involves going beyond logic so that the creative worker can bring insights that are not known to the world.

> Creativity without logic appears absurd to the world. Logic without creativity makes individuals merely conform to society. If we use creativity and scientific logic as two legs, we can run faster and deal with life affairs more efficiently.

The mind that does not care about evidence, logic, and what is known is free to jump from known to unknown. Dependence on doctrine, logic, or formulae makes the mind adhere to the known domains, and so that it is not free to generate creative output. If one uses old formulae or knowledge from books, it cannot be called creativity.

While your formulae and education are useful for catalysing your work, the most important thing for being creative is 'not depending on known information'. If you are able to go beyond science and technology, and if you are able to go beyond evidence, then it is possible to bring great insights into the world that have never been heard before. I am not advocating ignoring science. If creative insights are not explained in scientific terms, they look absurd to the world. An input from science is needed after having creative insight. If science demands evidence, however, then the facts that are also creative insights might be excluded.

*   *   *

Natural response evokes creativity

When man uses his intellect, he requires time to respond to situations and people because the intellect requires time to analyse information and make appropriate decisions. When the intellect is not involved in the process of creativity, time is not a factor in bringing about the creative response. Creativity is a process that functions outside of time. Man has an inherent ability to be creative and has the ability to express his creativity outside of time. However, we can notice the contamination of intellect when we feel that we need for time to resolve a situation. The decisions that we make spontaneously or the insights that we grasp instantaneously come to us when intellect and time factors are not hindrances to our way of life.

Unknown Truth of Life

When you respond to life situations naturally, and not according to scripture, teachers, belief systems, or intellectual propositions, you will identify your own nature, which expresses itself with effortlessly.

Such a natural response involves non-thinking and actions that emerge out of the psychological domain that is anonymous to man.

Natural responses to situations and people evoke natural actions that are spontaneous and that are the reflections of pure consciousness. Evoking such a response helps you to discover your own nature. Such actions are natural and true of their own accord, not according to a system of belief.

Approaching life's situations and other people naturally awakens your gifts, and your abilities. When you respond to situations naturally without using any fixed scheme to manipulate your response, your consciousness instantaneously becomes part of Nature in its entirety.

The 'Natural Response' does not involve fear about end results or flattering other people. The purpose of the natural response is to go beyond the abilities of the mind and evoke a creative response from yourself. Such responses from your original nature promote the growth of consciousness.

*   *   *

Vijay Pabbathi

Creativity dissolves the feelings of nationality

Joining in a political group to serve one's country, or joining a religious group, may give one a feeling that one is going in the right direction. While you as a person are desperate to serve your country or religion, you are trying to fit into a social pattern that brings personal accolades. You are also ignoring your natural abilities and capabilities when you give precedence to what society believes is right.

When man is not creative, he tends to use the name of his country as a means to attain pride, which will dissolve as soon as the individual is creative. So, basically, when people bluster with the pride of a nationalist outlook, it is an indication that these people are not using their own abilities – that is what I currently see in the world.

A genuine interest springs from offering a contribution by expressing who you are. When you find your creativity, your work will not be bounded by nationalities. Creativity dissolves national boundaries.

> Once you are able to bring something creative that has not previously been witnessed by the world, your mind will ignore the petty fights based on nationalities. Only then, will you be able to help yourself and others.

If you genuinely wish to help your country or people, the way to do so is to use your natural talents to contribute to your country or people. Such service will benefit individuals as well as the nations. Simply fighting with other people on the pretext of protecting your national flag, language, or country will add to the ashes. This is your decision.

* * *

What destroys creativity?

As I see it, understanding what destroys creativity is more important than following methods in order to be creative because understanding what destroys it provides the required clarity. Out of such clarity, man becomes intelligent and will have the capability to see the human problem beyond the dimensions of intellect. Without having such clarity, any techniques that we use to be creative will fail because we will be intellectual when we follow techniques. Intellectual affairs do not lead to true creativity.

If we do not understand how to deal with life situations, we cannot teach our children. When parents push their children to have ambitious plans, it outwardly appears as if they love their children, but inwardly it often serves their self-interest. When there is self-interest, how can love exist? A child raised under the guidance of ambitious parents finds it difficult to appreciate his or her own life. Thus the environment we develop in is sometimes counterproductive to understanding life. When ambition begins, life becomes compromised.

Titles and certificates might be valuable for earning a livelihood, but they are irrelevant to creativity. The urge to have certain experiences, certificates, or titles creates psychological demands that will eliminate creativity. When we push our children to earn certificates or be the best in a group, we unconsciously damage that child's creativity. Children who are brought up under psychological pressure to be the best at academics will remember their original interests and what they have lost at a later point in their careers if they follow their parents' path for them.

Organisations or research institutions that are seeking creative individuals will exclude men and women who have original talent by giving more importance to people with degrees or titles. Such an atmosphere will create a conditioning effect on both employers and employees with a net result of excluding originality. Certificates and titles have their own importance when certain expertise is needed. When creativity is being sought, however, emphasis on certificates becomes meaningless.

Competition can never make man creative, and indeed, it destroys creativity. The need to win in a competition exposes you to a tremendous psychological pressure, which makes you unintelligent and provides an unconscious escape route from being creative.

> Competition and creativity are mutually exclusive. When you feel competitive with others, you cannot generate creative output. It is also true that when you have creative output, you will not feel the need to compete with others.

A society that respects certificates excludes creativity. When a person unconsciously gives more importance to certificates and titles, original talents will be excluded. This is one of those factors that mean that a person will accomplish only a fraction of what they could achieve in this situation.

A mind cannot be creative while at the same time experiencing fear. Fear and creativity are mutually exclusive and cannot exist in the same psychological space. Fear is one of those side effects that we get when we depend too much on intellect. The intellect cannot get rid of fear. The intellect can help you to pilot an aeroplane or perform a difficult surgical operation, but it cannot make you creative, as fear comes along with the use of intellect.

The 'attitude of linear progress' will create time-bounded pressure to obtain certain outcomes and engender constant fear. On that basis, a man who is impatiently trying to get certain end results will not achieve creative output.

The mind depends on past knowledge and learning experiences that help man to survive. It learns using every experience so that it can use the data to plan the future. Ideas take you on a guided tour in a known psychological space. To be creative, you need to explore the unknown domains of psychological space where there are no rules. Tapping the unknown has to be your own venture and journey.

Mind's ability to adhere to ideals depends on the strength of its conditioning effect or conviction about the ideal. All ideals disappear from the mind when a person is exposed to danger or natural calamities, or if basic requirements are not satisfied. For the minds of people who barely have enough daily bread, every meal is fulfilment and ideals mean nothing. The ideals play their role only when a person has disposable resources and time.

Ideals destroy creativity. Is this not so? Ideals make a thick fence between what is known and unknown. Ideals do not allow information to flow from the unknown to the known. When a person responds to a situation or people based on ideals, how can that person bring any creative output?

All psychological demands block creativity, irrespective of one's academic and cultural background. When the outcome is irrelevant, only then does the mind receive creative insights from the unknown psychological domains.

A psychological demand can be anything related to life affairs. Some examples are a demand to achieve certain results or to meet the requirements of one's partner or organisation. All psychological demands make the mind wander in known areas and consider definitive formulae that provide predictable results. These psychological demands indirectly generate fear and therefore the mind cannot leave the known secured psychological spaces.

If you are able to perfectly relax without any deadlines to finish a task, the quality of mind changes. When you lose track of time, when you are not concerned with deadlines, then the quality of your mind changes. Based on my personal experience, the time-bound consciousness hinders creativity.

*   *   *

Trap of 'difficult is right'

The most difficult thing in man's life is following what appears to be the 'easy way' – because 'accomplishing difficult things' is respectable in our society. We have developed a society in which reputation or applause depends upon doing something difficult. We see this in news reports, world records, film stories, and so on. We unconsciously think that achieving difficult things is right.

Why do we assume that 'difficult is right'? This is because when man achieves a difficult thing, there is applause, which gives pleasure. For man, who craves pleasure, anything that provides pleasure is perceived as truth, whether the situation is true or not. Because the pleasure is the measure, the activity that gives the pleasure becomes true and justified in man's thinking – that is the basis of delusion. The support from society or a group of people gives extra emphasis – reinforcement – of the same delusion. Since the achievements that are based on making the effort are highly applauded in society, this misconception is seen as truth.

The perception is that happiness for man depends on the credo 'difficult is right' and 'easy is wrong'. If someone provides easy solutions, our minds regard them as useless. For man, the complexity of the task is proportional to the intensity of the resultant happiness. By following the paradigm that difficult is right, man struggles to accomplish difficult tasks and by so doing excludes his creative abilities.

Except for man's thinking, everything in nature follows the path of least resistance, based on a variety of natural examples. For example, an electric charge always moves in the path of least resistance, whether the charge is observed in living or non-living systems. Water moves toward the path of least resistance in both living and non-living systems. It is possible to find a wide range of examples of this principle, if one is interested in this subject.

Man has created a society in which individuals who can perform difficult tasks get the highest reputation, and most awards and laurels. Since accolades and respectability are associated with performing difficult things, man tends to make everything difficult for his own self-gratification. This process leads man to waste his creative energies in exchange for laurels. Unless you are aware of the original price of the laurels, you will try to seek the laurels while assuming that winning laurels is equivalent to discovering the truth. This is one of the reasons why man might accomplish only a fraction what he is capable of accomplishing.

When a mind struggles against resistance, it struggles against the body because the body follows natural laws. Despite the struggle, the mind does not follow the least-resistant pathway. This is because the mind believes that greater activity of the mind is proportional to happiness. If the mind accepts lesser resistance, the brain has less activity and therefore the mind concludes that following the path of least resistance is incorrect.

In my understanding, human minds follow the pathway of high resistance and exchange the 'perception of feeling good' at the cost of being intelligent and creative. In other words, the mind likes to go against natural directions because the mind perceives that 'difficult is right', whereas nature perceives that 'easy is right'. Such perceptions of the human mind are built into the nature of our minds. If man is able to recognise this limitation in his own mind, he breeds a new civilisation that harmonises the natural forces with effortless ease.

A man who tries to accomplish something wherein within his success it is difficult to gain social applause, he will waste tremendous psychological energy. It is impossible to be creative while the mind wastes psychological energy in achieving difficult things. By doing difficult things, you may get something according to your personal choices, but you will not bring something that world has never seen it before. When difficult things are appreciated in our society, do you have the courage to go against the social norm and break away from the false? That is your decision.

*   *   *

Vijay Pabbathi

Physiological limitation

The mind depends on external divisions. A division could be religious, political, social, economic, or intellectual. The idea of division or classification is important to the mind because it has to process so much information in order to make decisions. In evolution, this attribute is acquired for the purpose of survival. For example, for survival, it is necessary to classify whether situations are dangerous or safe.

The processing of information by the mind depends on enhancing contrast. For example, it cannot perceive a white line on a white background. In order to see and understand the information about a white line, it has to be drawn upon any contrasting colour. Unless there is a contrast, the mind cannot recognise sensations like touch, smell, vision, and taste. For example, one can hear sound only when there is silence in the background. The property of recognition itself is entangled with expressing the divisions in everything we perceive.

In fact, the property of recognition has been developed in evolutionary terms to recognise the difference between pain and pleasure. Disappearance of these differences is detrimental for the existence of a species. For example, if man cannot feel pain, he cannot spot life-threatening dangers. If man cannot have pleasure, what drives the sexual emotions? I therefore suggest that the idea of making divisions with the mind is a natural process.

My emphasis is that the perceptions of being distinguished are exaggerated perceptions that are already present at a functional level of the mind.

As long as the mind maintains its functional patterns, as described above, its activities intrinsically involve distinctions like good/bad, success/failure, and so forth. Man cannot perceive good unless there is a bad in the background. If there is only good luck available in the world, how do you perceive the good luck as such? This is a natural aspect of the human mind. Good luck can be perceived only when there is no good luck in the backdrop. The mind cannot perceive situations or circumstances in any other way.

*   *   *

Applications

1. I will explore whether my mind can be creative and express the natural abilities that emerge when I am being anonymous.

2. I comprehend that being creative does not require me to accomplish difficult tasks. I, therefore, will not jeopardise my life by undertaking ambitious tasks. Instead, I will investigate whether effortless actions can naturally lead me to be a creative person.

3. I understand that responding to situations naturally opens new doors in my consciousness and awakens a creative response.

4. I will not worship logic (reason). Instead, I will use logic when needed. In this way, I will achieve the highest possible progress in both the personal and the professional level.

*   *   *

5. Living in Your Own Life

Insights

When man expresses creativity, he has the possibility of ending the desperate struggle to be successful in a competitive society. Having flexible goals leads man to incorporate creative solutions in dealing with both personal and professional affairs.

Changing the course of action according to the emerging facts of life permits individuals to naturally succeed in life. Man develops important cognitive skills, which are essential for him to deal with life intelligently, if his goals are to adapt to the emerging facts of life.

In a nutshell

When your goals are flexible, you will unconsciously give importance to life and will see what is natural to you.

The most common goals for modern man are: reaching one of the top positions in his field; drawing the highest salary; achieving a good reputation; being highly respectable in society; or attaining security for life. Most of us want to pursue such goals. In doing so, we set fixed goals and we call them our dreams. Since we want to accomplish something so desperately, we tend to adhere to these fixed goals and use them to drive our lives, and spend our resources and time to achieve these fixed goals. In attaining the fixed goals, regardless of the nature of the goals, are we missing anything valuable in our lives? Are we trying to chase our dreams in exchange for something more valuable than achieving the dreams?

Our goals usually depend on certain demands from life. The nature of this demand may be related to pleasure, satisfaction, knowledge, wealth, personal requirements, or fulfilment. These demands can also be related to financial, political, religious, personal, academic, or social factors. Regardless of the nature of our goals, however sacred or respectable they may be, we need to ask ourselves: Are we living for our goals? What is happening to our lives while we are meeting all these psychological demands and urges? Is there anything valuable that we are losing without knowing it, with the pretext of accomplishing psychological security?

Let us understand what we lose from the way that we handle our life requirements and goals. It is important to discover whether we are simultaneously missing something valuable while we are pursuing these fixed goals. Once we understand the missing piece of information, we will be able to set goals intelligently that do not take away anything from our lives.

* * *

The weakness of the mind has to be carefully understood if you are interested in living your own life. If the mind is confused and is incapable of being intelligent, then everything that we perceive will be under suspicion. One such weakness sprouts when we try to accomplish 'what we should be' or 'what we want' as opposed to seeing 'what it is' and 'what I am'. Let us verify the quality of our mind.

It is normal that we fix our goals when we want to accomplish something of our choosing. Fixed goals create time-bounded pressure on the mind and create a psychological demand to accomplish the results within a certain time frame. The process results in fear about the end results. The moment there is fear, the mind becomes incapable of seeing the facts within situations as they are. So, the root cause of an inability to see the facts as they are is based in our nature of having fixed goals. Let us also see how the natural mechanisms are operating before we make a decision about the best possible ways to deal with the problem.

* * *

Vijay Pabbathi

Nature's way

I will use a natural example that is related to maintaining the body's balance to explain my insight into the context of how nature handles goals. The human body always tries to maintain its bodily functions in a state of equilibrium or balance (technically known as *homeostasis)*. The purpose of maintaining the body in a state of equilibrium is: a) to meet the body's requirements; b) for survival; and c) to maintain a neutral physiological environment so that all of the body's other organs function at their best.

In the process of maintaining balance within itself, the body observes its requirements for what needs to be done in a given situation. For example, if a person is running, the heart must pump more blood to the muscles to meet the requirements of the body. When a person is sleeping, the muscles do not need more blood, so the heart does not beat as fast.

Let us understand a natural situation of the human body. First, there is *'true observation' (the fact)* about the requirements of the body, and the body changes its goals according to true observation to maintain its health. The two key points in this mechanism are finding facts and developing adaptable goals based on those facts.

The observation must be true and the goal must be flexible. If one of these factors fails, the body loses equilibrium and then disease begins. For example, if the body fails to recognise its ever-changing needs, disease can begin. If the body sets a fixed goal and circumstances change, disease can begin. The body functions this way for every millisecond, from birth to death. The mechanism just explained has been oversimplified, to describe the relevant points in the context of this chapter.

The above example suggests that natural mechanisms contain recognisable facts from each situation *and have adaptable (flexible) goals that follow the facts.* In my understanding, both factors are useful to apply to real life situations.

*   *   *

Miracle of flexibility in goal-setting

Man is keen to have miraculous solutions in his actions. He has fixed goals and tries to achieve fixed outcomes. When we want a fixed outcome, naturally we make much effort in accomplishing the outcome of our choice. Thus, miracles cannot happen whenever a fixed solution is sought. My emphasis is that we exclude the miraculous solutions from the outset by the very nature of our requirement to have a fixed outcome. The choices we make and miracles are mutually exclusive.

> Flexible goals engender creative output. The only way to see the miraculous (creative) outcome in our endeavours is to incorporate flexibility in what we want.

If you are not interested in seeing natural solutions in your endeavours, this description might be quite boring. On other hand if you wish to explore what is naturally yours in your life situations, being flexible in your goals could be tool to discover remarkable outcomes.

The mind always looks for certain end results as soon as there is a goal to achieve. If the goals are fixed, the end results will also be fixed. The goal itself is often structured to achieve fixed end results. Therefore the mind unconsciously perceives only the information that is relevant to the goals. In other words, the mind ignores facts if they do not fit with the expected end results. Once man aims for a fixed goal, the remaining process of filtering facts happens unconsciously because the very nature of intellect is to process data that is relevant to the expected outcome. When the mind ignores facts, it becomes unintelligent.

If the goal is adaptable or flexible, the mind cannot unconsciously filter the facts. If the goals are flexible, the end results become flexible as well. The process also eliminates time-bounded pressure and fear about end results. Thus, having flexible goals indirectly eliminates fear about the end results.

Upon having flexible goals, psychological demands disappear – therefore the fear about the outcome disappears. Once there is no fear, the mind is better able to assess the facts from situations and people. Thus, the quality of the mind changes as soon as the goals are flexible.

If the mind is continuously adapting to seeing the facts without projecting what it wants, man can develop new cognitive skills to handle life affairs more intelligently because the very nature of adaptability allows the mind to calculate and accomplish results without conscious effort.

> A man who is keen to respond to the facts as opposed to a man who is struggling to accomplish his own dreams will have an evolutionary advantage in terms of accessing the best possible opportunities.

If goals are fixed, the intellect makes every effort to bring the expected outcome within a certain time period. When goals are flexible, the role of the intellect is diminished. If the focus of the intellect is directed to finding the facts by having flexible goals, the intellect has to wait until the facts are discovered. In this way man drives the intellect rather than being driven by it. The insight of having flexible goals brings tremendous psychological change in the way we deal with our life affairs.

* * *

Flexible goals reveal 'natural solutions'

For example, if you obtain a job without any effort from your intellect, it is likely that you will not constantly struggle to maintain your position. Indeed, you will be happy and peaceful in using a skill that comes naturally to you. The question is: how do you seek something that comes naturally? What is the secret of having such job or relationship or achievement?

If you are looking for a fixed solution using a fixed goal, you will not see what is natural to you. The only way to see 'what it is' is to stop projecting 'what it should be'.

> The approach of having flexible goals and changing your course of action according to the emerging facts of life permits individuals to naturally succeed in life.

Our intellect cannot comprehend nature's plans from the outset. Therefore, it is normal that most of us do not have flexible goals. However, if you look at natural evolution, you will notice that the entire survival of a species depends on their adaptability to their environment.

Nature's way begins to follow a certain direction and changes direction according to facts (pure observation). The situation is the same whether the system is inside or outside of the skin. If flexibility, which is the most important quality of nature, is not built into our plans, we may terminate our own existence.

*   *   *

Flexible goals evoke creativity

As mentioned in the above section, if you have a fixed goal, you will end up with a fixed solution. How can a fixed solution that you scheme about turn out to have a creative (unknown) solution? So the fixed goal (whatever we wanted) will exclude creativity. Is this not true? The central theme in this chapter, which is about having flexible goals, is not only related to our life circumstances, but is also important to scientists.

Many important discoveries in science and technology are serendipitous and are regarded as chance discoveries. As long as we have rigid goals, we need to depend on chance factors. It is possible to turn serendipity into a habit of making important observations by being flexible in what you are looking for. There is a famous saying by Louis Pasteur (French scientist, 1822–95): 'Chance favours the prepared mind'. How do you prepare your mind to discover your chances?

> If your goals are flexible, there is a
> possibility of discovering something
> totally new that is more suited
> to your needs than your personal
> choices.

I say that having flexible goals is a method of preparing your mind to discover something totally novel. If your goals are flexible and you are not trying to worship your choices, you will have the possibility of discovering something totally new that is more suited to your needs than your personal choices. Unless you have a flexible mind, you will merely use science instead of contributing to science.

The mentality that craves serendipity is the mentality that sets fixed goals and destroys serendipity. You do not have to be a holy man to understand this fact. If you understand that your attitude of setting fixed goals is preventing you from having great discoveries, there is a greater possibility for having chance discoveries more frequently.

When the intellect is rigidly sought out to attack problems, your expectation is to have a conclusion for which you are looking. If you have the conclusion that you want, you simultaneously escape the creative outcome that exists beyond the intellect. Intellect will be extremely useful if it allows you to go beyond its use. If the knowledge that you have gained does not allow you to go beyond its use, there is no possibility to be creative individual.

When you are not creative, you will not find meaning in your own life and you will start peeping into others' activities. If you do not have any meaningful affairs, like producing creative output from your endeavours, you will start talking about something that gives you pride and jeopardise your own life and others.

Most of the people in society are serious about what they want and they have fixed goals to accomplish the desired outcome. If you go with flexible goals, you will be seen as insane and society will not respect the idea of having flexibility in your goal setting. So, society will push you and ridicule your attitude. If you do not conform to the norms of society, you will not be popular. Do you have the courage to be right at the cost of your reputation? Do you have the stamina to stand alone and be right in order to awaken your creativity and your natural abilities?

* * *

Many people spend their lives striving to achieve a high reputation or something that gives them pride or honor. A man who is hungry and does not have daily bread gives more importance to life than to these ideas. A hungry man sees that satisfying his hunger is life. It is the man who has disposable time and resources who thinks that 'living for ideas' brings fulfillment and therefore struggles to live for ideas.

When a man is hungry, there is no need to tell him about the importance of being flexible in his endeavors. This is because a hungry man will not survive unless flexibility is incorporated into his actions. It is common experience that we eat whatever is available when we are hungry. When the bladder is full and struggling to empty itself, we naturally do not care whether the toilet is clean. Rigidity in action is an intrinsic property of man's thinking when he is not struggling to survive. All the choices make man's life miserable when his ideas take priority over life. The flexibility in our actions depends on our state of mind, whose priorities are different when there is no need for survival.

Leading a life for the sake of ideas is a fundamental trap in man's thinking because ideas are not facts. These ideas have no natural existence. When children are exposed to ideas, they think that ideas like 'accomplishing honour' or 'striving to be a great person' are facts. Unconsciously, we lead our children to follow these ideas instead of leading them to follow real facts.

Living for these ideas is a film story. The film stories are meant to be unusual in order to achieve commercial success. When children see those films, they think that living for ideas is right.

> Many of us have been encouraged to live for pride or to imitate someone who is famous. It is highly applauded in society to do

something that brings fame – the whole circus is false and sabotages life.

We struggle to live for ideas until there is a spiritual breakdown, and then we look for a spiritual guru or saviour, assuming that someone else will help us. That is what usually happens to us.

An expert may be able to write about the philosophy of these ideas. All such academic information merely gives a feel-good explanation. When the mind provides an activity with a 'feel-good explanation', it helps you escape from the facts. Once the mind finds psychological security in words and explanations, it does not look for facts – because security through words is perceived as truth, which is the basis of misleading perception. This is why it is important to look for the facts that exist beyond academic logic and beyond feel-good perceptions.

* * *

Applications

1. By having flexible goals, I will clearly see 'what I am' and what my natural skills are. Thus, the process of having flexible goals will lead me to find my own life as opposed to what I am expected to become.

2. Whenever I seek natural or creative solutions, I will incorporate flexibility into my expectations about the end results. I understand that this process will spontaneously make me creative and intelligent.

3. I realise that life is more important than struggling to live for ideas. I, therefore, will not be deluded by looking at others who try to become famous or obtain power.

*　　*　　*

6. Being Intelligent

Insights

Observing the facts from everyday life affairs is a means of making the mind intelligent. If man knows how to find the facts from everyday life affairs, all the conflicts, confusions, and uncertainties will disappear without struggling to follow any technique.

In a nutshell

It is the way of life that makes man to unconsciously recognise facts and deal with life affairs intelligently.

Vijay Pabbathi

Intellect and intelligence

The process of becoming an intellectual being involves learning how to reason, making hypotheses, calculating, speculating, estimating, comparing, discussing, evaluating, analysing, drawing conclusions, and so on. Time is required to produce logic. Intelligence comes into being when the mind unconsciously recognises the facts and responds with an immediate action. Such responses do not involve time lapse. Since logic is not required and non-thinking is involved in the process of discovering facts, the time factor is irrelevant. Intellects require time, because the process of intellect requires ideas and processing data over a period of time. Therefore intellect cannot respond spontaneously, whereas intelligence expresses an immediate action in response to seeing the facts.

Intelligence is characterised by an immediate action. For example, the moment of seeing a tiger is juxtaposed by the action of escape. You do not need to plan the escape. Escape happens, even before the mind brings the idea, if the mind sees the danger as a fact.

Intellect has its own place in the development of science and technology, which makes man's life comfortable. Because the intellect has been so useful to man, he overemphasises the intellect. Certificates and title are involved in intellect. Certificates do not help you to deal with life efficiently. Certificates represent technical expertise and intellect. For example, you may be one of the best doctors, pilots, engineers, or accountants. Your expertise, titles, and certificates do not represent intelligence or how efficient you are in handling your own life affairs.

Intellect requires effort to produce efficiency. Effort excludes the observation of facts. Competition requires effort and stimulates the intellect, and it does not generate intelligence. Extraordinary transformation comes into being by our seeing the facts as they are and not by struggling to achieve fixed goals.

When the intellect intrudes before discovering the facts, actions are delayed. Such a delay is characterised by arguments, demand for justification, and suspicion about what actions to take.

The intellect serves hopes, psychological securities, and comforts. Intelligence makes you a better human being and solves life's problems efficiently. A man without intelligence is poised to destroy himself. If the mind is vigilant and keen to see the facts beyond hopes and meeting psychological urges, it become intelligent. Such intelligence exists in its own right, not according to intellectual theories, scriptures, and justifications.

Imagine that a full stomach rejects food and an empty stomach accepts food. That means an empty stomach that shows its craving for food ignores everything except food. A full stomach also ignores everything including the food. The body's organs show something as a fact based on their requirements, regardless of the reality of the situation. A human mind also follows the same rule. It ignores the facts when demands are satisfied and stops seeing the facts that may lie beyond its requirements.

If one is interested in observing the facts in life affairs, it is important to see beyond psychological security and the activities that engender hopes. If you are able to see the nature of psychological demands before serving those demands, your mind will deal with problems intelligently.

A man who experiences psychological demands or frustration also misses the facts. When man has troubles, he gets frustrated, which makes the mind unable to see the facts. The mind becomes intelligent – not by meeting its demands – but by seeing the nature of urges.

Whenever man conceives a goal, time-consciousness and fear about the end results will be conceived simultaneously. Regardless of the nature of the goal and academic and cultural backgrounds, man breeds a time-bounded pressure and fear about the end results simultaneously.

These three factors influence one another, with or without conscious control. Interestingly, dissolving the time factor eliminates the fear about the end results. You can experience this in your own life affairs. For example, if you drop the deadline in the middle of serious pursuits, you can feel how much psychological relief you experience.

Importantly, time-bounded thinking excludes the ability to look at the facts as they are. It is impossible to see the facts in an artificial time-scale. When the goals become more important than life, personal hurry is inevitable and our own attitudes set the stage for escaping from facts.

*   *   *

How to perceive the facts

Most of us assume that the perception of facts is an intellectual affair because we often observe facts in scientific experiments – therefore we think that we can also observe the facts that are required for dealing with life efficiently in this way. That perception is right, without doubt, as far as laboratory experiments are concerned. Man can discover facts using the intellect when it is used outwardly. However, the intellect is not useful for perceiving facts that require dealing with life efficiently. This is primarily because the nature of intellect is entirely differently when it is used outwardly and when it is used inwardly.

Where the perception of facts that are related to life events is concerned, intellect is misleading to man because the intrusion of intellect excludes the unconscious grasping the facts. Grasping facts with the mind is an event like blood circulation or respiration in the human body. There are many millions of events within the body that occur without our knowledge. In the same way, the mind has to grasp facts in order to deal with life affairs intelligently.

Man has the unconscious ability to find the facts from situations or events. That unconscious ability is excluded as soon as man is desperate to achieve something. Thus, man loses important skills as long as he sets fixed goals and chases dreams. Please find this out for yourself, as there is no need to take my understanding as if it is yours.

Since grasping facts is not an intellectual faculty, we need to know how we can improve the intelligence of the mind so that the mind can unconsciously identify the facts. If *the way of life* is based on the attitude of non-linear progress, having flexible goals without time-bounded pressure, without self-importance, and expressing natural abilities, the mind will spontaneously identify the facts without using a special technique. Other chapters in this book elaborate on this advice.

It is the *way of life* that enables man to recognise the facts from life events. For example, if you are already using your natural abilities for the way of your life, your mind is already relieved from constantly calculating and controlling. The state of mind that you acquire in return for the expression of natural abilities is the ideal state that can unconsciously find the facts.

If your goals are flexible, you will inevitably see the situations and people as they are, because your mind will not be struggling to achieve a fixed outcome. All your intellectual methods that make you intelligent will be doomed to fail if your goals are not flexible.

If you are not struggling to win laurels or trying to be a famous person, the importance of ideas is already dissolved, even before you use any technique. If you are not struggling to have linear progress, your mind will have no fear about the outcome. Therefore, there is no requirement for the flood of ideas.

Unknown Truth of Life

> The mind that follows the attitude of non-linear progress as the way of life has the ability to grasp facts unconsciously, without making it a special event.

Finding the facts cannot be a special event. If you make it special, you will need to use your ideas to do so. It is the most ordinary event. In fact, you should not be able to classify whether it is sacred or profane. Since the mind should not make it a special process, the art of finding the facts should function like a natural process, like your heart beating. For example, you will not notice your heart beating if everything about the heart is going all right. If your heart is beating in a special way, you will need to see a doctor, because beating in a special way is the characteristic of heart disease. Similarly, when the mind finds facts, you will not notice as a special event. If you did notice this as a special event, you are not discovering facts. Based on that reasoning, if you are trying to learn a technique to identify facts, it will become an arduous process. The mind has to unconsciously recognise facts based on your way of living, like your heart beating.

*   *   *

Vijay Pabbathi

What destroys the ability to find facts?

An accumulation of more ideas and recalling ideas does not represent intelligence. Sharpening the mind to improve expertise is not related to intelligence. Using thought to change thought cannot make the mind intelligent. If you really want to change the quality of mind, you have to develop a serious interest in observing facts.

Ideas exclude discovering facts. An idea, regardless of the scientific advances that it is capable of creating, cannot help in finding facts. Ideas and facts share the same psychological space. They exclude each other. To observe a fact, the mind has to be uncluttered. The empty psychological space is an invitation to facts. A mind full of ideas is useless for finding facts.

Ideas may be useful for explain facts, once the facts are found out. However, they are detrimental to finding facts. When ideas die, the facts appear. You do not need to kill all your ideas forever, but to find the facts, the ideas have to take the back seat. The ideas have to follow the facts – not vice versa.

If we make an observation based on our beliefs, dogma, doctrines, systems, teachers, or opinions, we will not be able to identifying the facts (truth). If you are trying to prove something, your mind is incapable of discovering true observations (the truth). This is because it is an intrinsic limitation of the human mind that unconsciously escapes from the psychological space that is required to make a true observation.

Unknown Truth of Life

Facts are not based on the following factors:

1. Psychological demands/urges/securities
2. Time-bounded pressure
3. Effort, struggles, or goals
4. Fear or anxiety
5. Gurus, organisations, or an expert
6. Hypotheses, beliefs, or dogma
7. Intellectual projections and justifications

The effort to prove your ideas will sabotage you from discovering the facts. If you find a fact, the does not need to be justified, whether is scientific, personal, or spiritual. You may struggle to formulate your theories by linking facts. The struggle is related to your ideas/hypothesis/theory, and it is not related to facts. Even if the whole world denies it, sooner or later, the facts cannot be hidden. Therefore, there is no need to ask other people's opinion about the facts.

Constant searches to accomplish something, regardless of the nature of achievement, create psychological demands and make the mind escape from the facts. It does not matter whether you are searching for treasure, a partner, or God. The search makes the mind focus on the target and unconsciously filters what it sees as fact, as opposed to reality. The mind cannot find the facts while it spends an enormous amount of energy in finding what it wants.

The mind perceives satisfaction when it gains a number of supporters to sustain its beliefs. If there are no supporters to strengthen beliefs or ideas, the mind perceives this as an upsetting situation, as it has to discard the old beliefs and start accumulating new data. Thus, the reality of the way the mind functions is generally based on its nature of activity rather than the truth of the situation.

Numbers create a mesmerising phenomenon to the mind. For example, if millions of army men are marching, this suggests that they must be right. They appear to be right, not because what they follow is right but because the numbers, parades, and music create a hypnotic situation in which the mind loses itself. Whether it is a religious rally or political rally, the pattern of mind is the same.

Many people depend on others' views without thinking about it. Scientists, politicians, sportsmen, musicians, and religious leaders are examples. The dependence on the number of supporters is a social convenience when we have no ability to recognise the facts as they are. Facts do not depend on the number of supporters.

When you really – and not just in words – are able to see the facts as they are, you will leave your dress code and laugh at your own gestures of going around with an outfit of spirituality. As I mentioned, the mind has to grasp facts unconsciously. Any technique that you use to see facts will delude you because of the involvement of intellect.

*   *   *

Foundations of our thinking

I feel that understanding the nature of our perceptions helps us deal with life intelligently. Examining the foundations of our thinking is a wake-up call to get rid of delusions in our thinking and saves tremendous psychological energy that can be useful for sustaining our lives. Let me explain what foundations have helped me to understand life. If you examine what has helped me, it is possible that some of these foundations could be experimental tools to help you understand your own life.

Imagine that we have a beautiful building with outstanding design, a decent outlook, that is so appealing to the eye that it is regarded as one of the greatest buildings in the world. What good is that building without having the right foundation? What good is that building if it collapses internally? The foundation has to be right, and is more important than the external design, colours, and outlook. Nobody wants a building that collapses internally, regardless of its bewitching outlook. It appears to me that all of our technological advancements are like external outfits that make our lives comfortable and enjoyable, while our psychological perceptions are the foundations. Let us begin to lay the foundations of our thinking.

1. The first foundation: *'If the profit is not our measure'.*

In order to understand the nature of our perceptions, we have to step out of the 'profit-oriented thinking'. As long as we are thinking within the boundaries of a value-based system, we will exclude certain facts that make us intelligent.

> Something that gives profit or incentive becomes truth, as opposed to the absolute truth, if we do not have the nerve to see outside of the boundaries of a 'value-based system'.

So the first foundation necessary to understand the certainty of life is that what generates incentive, or something that we like, is not necessarily true. If the profit is your measure, then life becomes uncertain because everything in the universe is discontinuous, including your profits.

You may gain your profits if you expand the pleasure element and provide the activities that generate pleasure to your customers. If you wish to apply the same logic to life, then the life becomes uncertain. The intellectual affairs that man uses in business are not the devices that can show the certainty of life.

2. The second foundation: *'If the pleasure is not our measure'.*

Psychological comforts make you impermeable to the facts of life, although they are valued in society. If you are serious about wanting to understand what brings certainty to life, your enquiry needs to go beyond psychological comforts. Otherwise, what gives pleasures to our senses might appear to be true, and we delude ourselves by merely projecting what we like.

When pleasure is not the measure, we will not try to maintain progress in linear fashion. If you are not trying to maintain continuous success or pleasure, you have nothing to complain about.

> The state of mind that is not complaining about 'what is natural' feels the certainty of life.

3. The third foundation: *'What society appreciates is not necessarily the truth'*.

We need to investigate the facts of life, whether they are respected in our society, because our interest is not to fit the facts according to what society appreciates. What we are going to discover may be or may not be congruent with social conventions.

The facts do not depend on society; rather, society should depend on facts. For example, society cannot change the shape of the earth or the rotation of the earth. A true observation (fact) cannot be modified even if millions of people do not accept it. Truth simply does not necessarily depend on the number of supporters it has.

It is a norm in society that we depend on a number of supporters to elect a Prime Minister or President. It is also a norm in the legal system that the judge cannot decide whether a criminal deserves a punishment in most serious crimes, so the court depends on the jury. Thus society appreciates something as a fact and depends on the number of voters or supporters to support a political or legal system.

> We have developed some conventions to live in a society and those conventions are not necessarily the facts. Unless we have the ability to grasp the facts that fall outside the scope of social conventions, we will not truly understand life.

Social conventions are like traffic rules. For example, we need to drive a car on left-hand side of the road in Britain and on the right-hand side in America. Similarly, several other countries have their own social conventions. However, it is important understand that social convention is not absolute truth.

The facts do not require others' opinions, and they are standalone, such as the rotation of the earth. The rotation of the earth does not require the gospels or chanting to show that it exists. You do not need a holy war to prove a fact. Facts do not require symbols, gospel, or trademarks. All such attributes serve to allay psychological insecurity for a man who is desperate to prove facts. The third foundation also suggests that we do not need the opinions of other people to justify facts.

When we do not try to fit facts according to social conventions or others' opinions, we will save tremendous psychological energy that could then be directed to sustain life. Such a mentality, which does not make an effort to mould life according to social expectations, automatically finds the certainty of life, as there is no struggle to meet the social requirements.

I have heard the example of *'fitting a square peg in round hole'*. If man fits a round peg in a round hole, he cannot develop an appreciation in society because there is no difficulty involved in doing so. On other hand, if he fits a square peg in a round hole, he can obtain applause from the society because it is uncommon to do so. It is important to recognise that what society appreciates can act as driving force to sabotage your own life. Whatever is unnatural can attract the masses' attention and mislead you as if it is true. We need an eye that can recognise whether what we do is genuinely true.

4. The fourth foundation: *'The menu is not the meal'.*

Most of us know that the words (descriptors) that we use to explain things or the mental processes behind doing so are different from the things that are described. Similarly, a menu does not give insight into the taste of an entree. A menu, however colourful it may appear, does not satisfy hunger. Many authors and philosophers frequently use this example. However, if we are going in a journey to understand our lives, it is extremely important to understand a life situation or fact based on 'what it is' rather than the vocabulary that describes it. As a priority, we should not get lost among theories and words. This is why I have to remember that 'the menu is not the meal'.

The only way to taste what I am saying is to experiment with the insights and see whether these insights are useful in your own life. As long as you do not experiment within your own experience, there is a possibility that you will get into arguments. If you experiment, it is highly likely that there is nothing to argue because you become an authority.

5. The fifth foundations: *'See beyond physiological ability'.*

As part of this journey, it is useful to verify the functional limits of our minds to see the truth of life. For example, when the stomach is empty, we may not appreciate the beauty of a flower. When the bladder is full and waiting to be emptied, we may not appreciate what is going on around us. Thus the body's requirements influence what we see. When the bladder is empty and the stomach is full, people may like to talk about ideals, though that interest will disappear when the stomach is empty and the bladder is again full.

We see green leaves and assume that the colour of leaves is green. However, a green leaf does not appear to be green in the same way to a person who is colour blind as it does to one who is not. So, a person who cannot see the colour green can say that leaves are not green in colour. In fact, based on our physiological ability, we are able to recognise some colours, and therefore we tend to give names to what we see. A fact cannot be modified based on an observer's physiological ability to recognise fact.

My emphasis is that, if we cannot see certain facts, we have to accept our limitations, and we cannot argue about the absolute truth. Not seeing the facts that exists beyond our physiological abilities does not create problem if we understand our limitations. It is unintelligent to be carried away in this journey without addressing the limits of our cognitive abilities.

6. The sixth foundation: *'If we are not hopeful about the outcome'.*

Whenever we hope for certain end results, we unconsciously select information that supports our objective. Thus there is a danger that we will unconsciously ignore the facts of life. This is not our fault. It is an intrinsic inability of our thinking process that we cannot be hopeful and simultaneously perceive facts. When we hope to accomplish a certain outcome, we are naturally biased toward selecting the information that reflects our desires. I am not suggesting that one should not try to find hope. My emphasis is that facts exist beyond meeting the psychological demand for hope. If you are serious about finding facts, you need to have a keen eye to see the reality of existence beyond psychological demands.

Whenever there is a psychological insecurity, man seeks hope. This is the kind of thinking process we have. We therefore need to know the limits of our thinking.

7. The seventh foundation: *'If we are psychologically independent'.*

Many of us are dependent on one or other system of spiritual practices, based on various reasons within various cultures. Dependency on spiritual systems is highly valued by society. If you are dependent on one of those systems and lead your life according to its rules, the adherents of your system will respect you.

One of the major problems with any system of practice is that adherents are psychologically limited within the confinements of that system of practice. If we do not have the ability to step outside the zones of spiritual systems, our enquiry will be limited within the confinements of the information provided by religions or spiritual practices.

Importantly, if we do not have the ability to see life outside the framework of spiritual entanglement, it is all right as long as we accept that our understanding is not absolute. However, man is inescapably deluded if he assumes that what he practices is the absolute truth.

> Understanding life requires being detached from scientific and spiritual projections.

Our attachment to one of those faculties limits our thinking and we may unconsciously fit facts into our system of belief according to our interests. It is important to observe the nature of our thinking without craving to justify theories.

Imagine the way that one understands life when one lives with one's parents in contrast to one's understanding when one does not depend on one's parents. As long as you are dependant on your parents, regardless of the guidance that you have received from your parents, your understanding of life is limited. Your understanding of life exponentially grows when you do not need parental support. As long as one lives as a dependant of one's parents, he cannot see what kind of life experiences are excluded. The only way to see what life has to offer beyond what parental guidance offers is to step outside the home and start living autonomously. Living autonomously does not mean that you are disrespecting your parents, however.

Similarly, I recommend stepping outside the confinement of spirituality and intellectual affairs, and then investigating what you will discover about your life. Such understanding will sustain itself on its own accord, without having psychological dependency on any authority. When you are psychologically independent and deal the life affairs naturally, based on your own nature, you will become your own authority. Going away from your spiritual heritage, similar to my above analogy, does not mean becoming anti-system. It simply means that there is a growth within your consciousness and psychological maturation.

It is not important whether one agrees with the above-mentioned foundations. If our thinking is not limited by these factors, we can deal with life more intelligently. Even if we cannot use these insights, it is all right as long as we are aware of the limits of our perceptions. Such understanding helps us to develop whatever helps us in our lives.

Applications

1. I will investigate how to glean facts from life situations and people. I will begin exploring whether my way of life is helping me to recognise facts.

2. Whenever I rush in life circumstances, I will be aware that I am not dealing with the facts of life. I therefore will not be worried about delays in my daily life situations.

3. I see that the facts do not need to be supported by a number of people. Therefore, I need not regard the opinions of people as facts.

* * *

7. The Ultimate Purpose of Life

Insights

Innate abilities are natural and congenital abilities, and man acquires them from an source that is not known to the human intellect. Man naturally acquires an innate ability, just like his unique finger print, which is a gift from Nature.

The expression of innate ability is a means of fulfilling the ultimate purpose of life. Innate ability is not what 'you should be' – it is 'what you are'. It is the truth about you.

In a nutshell

Nature instils unique skills in every person to fulfil its purpose. Using your natural ability brings fulfilment and joy.

Regarding the purpose of life, most of us depend on the opinions of others. There are so many books and so many spiritual and religious teachings about the purpose of life. Is there a real purpose of life, not according to the books or other people, but according to Nature's Intelligence? The real purpose that I am keen to inquire into is not in accord with the explanations that are offered by my intellect. I am aware that the true purpose will be excluded when the intellect intrudes to describe the purpose of life. I am therefore not inclined to give you an intellectual proposition.

Man always says: *'I want to do this'* or *'I want to do that'*. In saying so, man makes an effort to accomplish *'what one should do'*. By achieving what one should be, can man have an ultimate achievement in life? By ignoring what you are, and how your natural abilities can help in your life, can you find the purpose of life?

Man is always passionate to find something that gives ultimate ecstasy. Man wants to accomplish that ultimate dream and put an end to all misery, petty fights with others, and all the competitive affairs in society. Is it possible for man to accomplish something that allows him to say *'this is it; I have done it. I am living a life that serves its purpose – this is my ultimate accomplishment'*? To arrive at such a state of mind, what is it that one should find?

How do we decide what is the ultimate purpose of life? If our decision is based on intellectual projections, then whatever is appealing to the mind appears to be meaningful. A patriot argues that serving the nation is the ultimate purpose of life. A scientist may argue that contributing to science may give an ultimate purpose of life. Similarly, people, based on their own religious beliefs, also suggest that following their respective master or gods gives ultimate purpose to life. I am not interested in using opinions or intellectual propositions to understand the true purpose of life. Instead, I am keen to inquire into the true purpose of everything in Nature so that the purpose of man's life can also be revealed. Such an enquiry negates the intellectual way of suggesting the purpose of life.

Surely the intelligence that has created man might have also given natural skills to him so that he can serve evolution while being part of it. What is that innate skill? Does such a skill exist? How do we discover it, if it does exist? This chapter provides some insights in these lines of inquiry.

*   *   *

Nature's way

Before discovering innate abilities, it is important to understand the nature of innate ability. I will use natural examples to explain innate abilities. For example, the heart uses its innate ability to pump blood to all parts of the body. It has to use its basic nature to be part of the system.

> In a healthy body, the goal of the individual organs is not to struggle to express the skills that they do not

have. Health happens to the body when organs express their innate (natural) abilities.

Innate ability can be demonstrated using any organ, cell, or system. For example, bones provide physical support and protect the vital organs. Bones also store important minerals like calcium and produce blood cells. Muscles provide movement and protection to other organs, and help regulate body temperature. The cells in the brain are part of the communication systems of the body, and also coordinate all bodily functions, which is crucial for survival. The lungs help to provide oxygen to the blood stream so that the blood can transport it to all other body parts. The stomach helps in the digestion of food and absorption of nutrients that are required for all other organs. Kidneys help the body in the excretion process, whereas the urinary bladder stores urine. Thus, every organ, cell, and system in the body has to use its natural abilities as part of the symbiotic process of maintaining health.

The organs achieve the end results without even struggling to compete for results. By doing so, any competition among the organs or systems disappears. There is no conflict in terms of their performances since they do not struggle to be distinguished.

Unknown Truth of Life

- ✓ Expression of innate abilities creates a simultaneous partnership (symbiosis) with every other organ in the body so that all other organs maintain the network of relationships in which none is greater than other.

- ✓ Expression of the innate abilities of organs does not create a power struggle or domination of one over another.

- ✓ Expression of the innate abilities of organs represents unnoticeable behaviour (anonymity). They disappear in silent function: we do not feel their presence if they are healthy. For example, you will remember your kidneys only if they become painful.

Health happens to the body when organs express their innate (natural) abilities. Thus, the innate abilities of individual body parts are spontaneously interconnected for their own welfare and for the welfare of the whole body. Innate ability is a skill that is present from birth. Its innate ability is a gift and is not something that is attained.

In health, every organ expresses its innate ability and has a partnership with every other organ so that the benefits of health are shared with all other organs. Thus the fulfilment happens to the body without even struggling to be healthy. The key point is that the organs do not need to accomplish anything that they do not naturally accomplish.

For example, fish swim – swimming is an innate ability of fish. A fish does not need training or user manual to learn to swim. A flower blooms – blooming is an innate ability of flower. No one needs to teach a flower to bloom. Similarly, innate ability is congenital, and the organs in the human body do not require user manuals or know-how before they express their function.

* * *

The situation of 'body parts in the entire body' is not unlike from the individuals in a society. We are part of Nature's Intelligence. Whether our minds accept it or not, our bodies receive energy in the form of oxygen and food from nature and contribute to the evolution of nature. The individual mind that perceives itself as separate from Nature's Intelligence is involved in a false perception. The reality is that no single individual can live without taking energy from nature. Thus, the intelligence within our body is interconnected with the intelligence that we see in the world.

From this, I came to understand that every person has an innate ability to express his innate skills as part of the natural process. Nature has a strategy for providing innate abilities that allow individuals to survive as part of the evolutionary process. Nature has already incorporated innate ability into every individual and the strategy is similar to the inclusion of innate ability in every seed.

Every person is unique in the same way that everyone has a unique fingerprint. A fingerprint is a representative example. Similarly, everyone has their own innate abilities. These abilities are dormant until we allow them to express themselves.

In using innate abilities, artists like painters, singers, and scientists tend to forget themselves and feel an inner silence. They disappear in silence while they use their own natural skills. If a person is using his natural abilities, there is no need to show a personal rush in his daily life because when you use your natural gifts, the intelligence of the entire universe functions to get thing right for you.

* * *

Innate ability: what is it not?

Innate abilities are not the projections of intellect. They cannot be taught by any academic programmes, as these abilities come to individuals at birth. However, education can be used to enhance the innate abilities that already exist.

Your innate abilities are independent of time and geography, and independent of external values like money, power, or family name. These skills are non-occult and are not intrinsic to any religions or spiritual groups. These skills can be utilised by individuals regardless of the time of day or year. They do not come by personal effort and therefore any external struggle to accomplish innate skill is a waste of time.

Intellect may help you to acquire skills by mechanical training, but it does not bring something from the unknown. However, such training may catalyse the expression of innate abilities if a person is fortunate to have an academic training in the area of skills that he already possesses. It is not the product of one's mind or man-made ideas. You cannot buy them with your money (even if you have a billion dollars).

Innate ability is a capability or a skill that is within you since birth. It is a gift that you have received from nature. However, occasionally, some people find careers in which their innate abilities synchronise with their academic abilities. Such situations help them to be outstanding achievers.

Innate ability is not an attribute of your titles or laurels. You will not find a user manual to identify this. You have to make your own manual.

* * *

Why innate abilities?

Using academic training, mankind has made many scientific advances. I suggest that what you have discovered using your intellect is a fraction of what you can discover using your innate abilities. This is because the psychological space that uses innate abilities uses natural forces that are part of Nature's Intelligence. Expression of innate ability not only opens new doors in your consciousness in which intellect has a limited role, but also helps individuals to be fulfilled.

Following your own nature (innate abilities) means that:

1. The energy used to express innate abilities does not come from your intellect or academic training. Your actions and endeavours are poised to be successful, as you will live in harmony with nature.

2. In using innate abilities, you are neither creating a cause and nor bringing the effect. You feel as if you are rising above the cause and effect relationship (Karma) because your expressions of innate abilities are nothing but the expression of Nature's Intelligence within you.

3. You will not make an effort to accomplish a specific outcome because expression of your natural gift or talent becomes the goal rather struggling to accomplish goals that are projected by the intellect or conditioned social

behaviour. Thus you will defocus from 'what you should be' and refocus on what you really are. The strategy helps you to navigate in a unique direction that is naturally yours.

4. You tend to relax frequently because all that you need to accomplish appears to be done by someone inside you. Inner peace becomes the central theme of your life.

> Using natural abilities brings fulfilment and joy in life, as the expression of innate ability is a process in which man harmonises himself with Nature's Intelligence.

Following your innate nature (calling your own nature) allows you to focus on your own skills rather than depending on others' skills. This strategy eliminates both individual struggle to accomplish and the competition in society. If you are using natural gifts, many problems of life disappear without you even trying to eliminate the problems.

How to discover innate abilities

Let us ask ourselves: how do we accomplish the growth of a seed? All we can do is arrange the conditions, such as providing good soil, irrigation, and allowing sunlight to let the seed grow. In a similar fashion, it is possible to provide circumstances that are conducive to expressing innate abilities. Since the expression of natural abilities depends on nature's gifts, we need to expose ourselves to the right conditions that harmonise with Nature's way.

You will need to identify the skills, abilities, expressions, or methods that are *not* the product of your intellect. If the mind is trained to perform a skill, how could you call that a natural ability? It is important to understand that natural ability is like gravitational force, which is not the invention of man.

There is no need to worship Nature to gain gifts from Nature. In fact, if you worship Nature, the distance between yourself and Nature remains the same forever. If you become part of Nature, you are Nature – therefore you will realise your innate abilities at the earliest opportunity. Becoming part of Nature means that you are also following natural laws as part of your life. Some of these laws, within the scope of this book, have been described.

Imagine that you are walking with a friend who is walking slowly. If you want to talk to him while walking together, you need to go at the same speed as him. If you walk slow or faster than your friend, you cannot talk to your friend. Similarly, if you wish to see your original nature, which is part of wider nature, then you need to move with Nature.

If you are in a rush (which could be based on what you wish to accomplish), you will also exclude the right conditions to identify your innate abilities. Therefore, utter relaxation on a regular basis is mandatory.

Is there anything that comes to your mind, and not because you have studied it as part of your education? A common mistake is that people will ignore whatever their ability gives them, without going through an arduous process of discovery. Easy things are useless for man, as I described in the other chapters. Nature does not give you useless things. Anything that has come to you without your working to achieve it must be treated as Nature's gift. I would pay the utmost attention to those skills or insights and work in the same direction to see whether your innate nature is part of those insights or skills. This is like using the flow of universal energy to reach your destination, with no personal struggle. Usually, we use natural skills during our childhood without having any professional training. Explore what you were good at as child to understand more about your abilities. Ask your mother and friends who witnessed your childhood to find out more about yourself.

Children's abilities are not usually contaminated by the intellect. It is useful to find out from your parents regarding your childhood interests. Your detailed account from your childhood would be beneficial and would provide some clues in discovering your innate abilities. Ask all of your family members to find out about your childhood behaviours. For

Unknown Truth of Life

example, my sister used to tell me that I would be a good teacher. I have never listened to her. After trying to achieve more in different fields, I finally settled on a career as a lecturer.

Hiding weaknesses delays the discovery of innate abilities. Hiding weaknesses wastes energy, and is the way to prevent the expression of your inner being. For example, if your seed is from an apple tree, let it express that. If your seed gives grapes, let it express that. Some people like grapes and others like apples. So what? The irony is that if you are a seed of an apple tree and you want to grow as a grape tree, the effort to become *'what you are not'* makes you neither *'what you are'* nor *'what you are not'*. That is what is happening in the world. That is why many people struggle in the world.

Many people do not realise their innate abilities and they try to set unnatural goals and waste their whole life to accomplish something for which their skills are not suitable.

> If you have a weakness that is born with you, then your weakness must have an evolutionary purpose that will help you to succeed in the world. Therefore, the chances of finding your innate abilities are high if you do not hide your weaknesses.

Whenever we face disappointments or dangers or difficult situations in life, we will do everything that is needed to escape from the situation, and then we generally do not pay attention to what skills we used to solve the problems. In my understanding, nature exposes you to danger for a reason. For example, some diseases come to children to increase their body's defence systems. Understand that disappointments and failures are raw materials that you can turn into opportunities. If you analyse how you transformed the useless situations into useful ones, you will become aware of your own alchemy, which was with your all the time. My emphasis is that you will miss the chance of finding your innate ability if you avoid the disappointments. Disappointments can be treated as raw material, if one is interested in finding facts, without any emotional reaction to the disappointments. This is because solving life problems brings unconscious energy from unknown source.

If you are struggling to accomplish success, that means you are not using your natural skills. When a person does not know his natural skills, he tends to struggle to accomplish something that has been projected by his mind. If a person has to observe what is natural to him, he needs to respond to situations naturally and see what unusual skills are being used in these life situations. Thus, 'responding to situations naturally' helps in discovering innate ability.

If you try to reach one of the top positions in society, you will accomplish 'what you should be', which may be different from 'what you are'. If your intention is to find your innate ability, you should not make an effort to be famous.

Unknown Truth of Life

If you are spontaneously being recognised without making any effort, that means you have already found your innate ability.

Imagine that a cow that is tethered cannot browse like a free cow that is left in an open field of grass. A cow that is not tethered to a fixed place can graze anywhere without any constraints. A cow that is tethered is constrained in its search for food and water. This is exactly what happens to man when his goals are fixed. If your goal is not flexible and you want something too desperately, it is unlikely that you will find your natural ability. To discover natural ability, your mind should be in a balanced psychological state that can recognise the facts. Your natural ability is a fact. If the mind is not intelligent to recognise facts, how can you recognise your innate skills? Therefore it is important to create a psychologically balance environment so that the mind can function intelligently. As mentioned previously, the moment goals are flexible, the quality of mind changes.

> If your goal is not flexible and you
> want something desperately, then
> it is unlikely that you will find your
> natural ability.

All of your knowledge will catalyse the expression of your innate ability if you already know what it is or if you have already started expressing it. However, your knowledge does not help you in discovering your innate ability. In fact, during a discovery phase, the knowledge we have gained hinders us in finding our innate ability, as we are reluctant to discard what we have gained.

The mind might have invested a lot energy and time in getting certificates, laurels, degrees, and awards. The more degrees you have, the more difficult it is for you to ignore the mind. This is why it is easier for students or young people who are in an early stage of life to investigate their innate abilities than it is for an expert in a particular field.

It is an arduous process for experts because the mind that has invested in training and that worships logic and ideas. The intrusion of ideas excludes the discovery of nature's skills. What you have learned will be useful for catalysing your natural skill if you combine your expertise in the area in which your natural skills are involved.

In summary, some of the key points in discovering innate abilities are:

1. finding out childhood interests,
2. not hiding the weaknesses,
3. resolving the disappointments,
4. being anonymous,
5. being flexible with goals,
6. not rushing to meet life requirements, and
7. responding naturally to situations.

Unknown Truth of Life

Some questions to ask yourself:

1. Are you trying to imitate someone else's work?
2. Are you making an effort to accomplish an outcome?
3. Are you feeling bored in your work?
4. Are you in a rush to achieve results?
5. Do you want someone to appreciate your work and thus decide the quality of the work?
6. Are you feeling competitive with others to achieve an outcome?
7. Are you being affected by peer pressure in your endeavours?
8. Are you interfering with other people's nature in accomplishing your goals?
9. Does your work involve demanding things from other people or controlling others?
10. Are your goals more important than your life?

The answer to the above questions is 'No' for those people who have found their innate abilities.

11. Is your work providing satisfaction in such a way that you are not looking for another profession?
12. Can you reproduce your work irrespective of your nationality or cultural or religious background?

The answer to the above questions is 'Yes' for those people who have found their innate abilities.

Vijay Pabbathi

* * *

There are many stories available in literature to stimulate you to be successful. Such stories often show how a poor boy or girl who did not have daily bread began a career by selling newspapers and finally became a president of their country. Such stories may boil your blood and project false plans regarding what you should be. My concerns are deeper than making you successful and are associated with evoking what you naturally are. This is why the examples that I am using are related to natural abilities that do not fit with traditional success stories.

I have noted many examples in which individuals used their innate abilities. Dr. Frank H. Netter (1906–91, born in Manhattan – an artist and physician) had a family that disapproved of a career as an artist and influenced him to study medicine at New York University. As a student, he used to help his professors by painting pictures of human anatomy. When he finished, he used his medical art to supplement his income and produced nearly 4,000 illustrations. Now all over the world his paintings have been used by doctors and medical students. Although he became a doctor, he used his own abilities to complement his profession.

You become more productive when
you use your natural skills which are

Unknown Truth of Life

generally ignored when your goals
are fixed.

Sting is an English musician from Newcastle-upon-Tyne. His full name is Gordon Matthew Thomas Sumner. He wanted to be a musician. His life circumstances made him a teacher and he worked as a teacher in Cramlington for two years. He followed his interests part-time and started performing on evenings and weekends. Now he is universally known as Sting. His skills are independent of his credentials and his academic background, which suggests that the expression of innate abilities do not necessarily require academic credentials.

I have heard that Joanne Rowling (born in South Gloucestershire, England) was originally unemployed and lived on state benefits. She used skills that are not gained by an academic background and wrote the Harry Potter series. My emphasis is that you do not need user manuals or academic training to produce the world's best work if you are depending on your innate skills. If the innate abilities are dependent on the credentials that a person can accumulate, then the individuals working in one of the reputed universities should have written the Harry Potter series.

Michael Faraday (born in London, England, 1791–1867) was a great experimental physicist and was the discoverer of electricity. He did not have any user manuals to produce the electricity. At the age of fourteen, he apprenticed to a book binder and earned money by lending out newspapers. In his later life, he did his own experiments and discovered electricity. I have heard that Michael Faraday had many disappointments in his life, as he was not even considered a 'gentleman' in those days. In the UK, his photo has been used on the £20 note. Achieving the most credible work does not require your pride, power, or wealth. If external values are required to produce such a great work, then the King of Arabia or another wealthy person should have discovered electricity.

Sir William Herschel (born in Hanover, Germany, 1738–1822) was an oboist in a travelling orchestra. He built his own telescope as a part-time interest and discovered Uranus. He was an astronomer for the King of England. In the later part of his career, he also contributed to the discovery of infrared radiation. If you think carefully how an oboist could discover the planet Uranus and help discover infrared radiation, it appears to be a most absurd story.

> The innate skills given to each individual have a universal role in fulfilling their potential. Thus, your expressions have a greater cause in the whole universe.

Unknown Truth of Life

Srinivasa Ramanujan (Tamil Nadu, India, 1887–1920) did not have formal training in pure mathematics though he made many contributions to mathematics. His brilliant work was recognized at the University of Cambridge. His work was highly unconventional and natural to him. Recently, in the field of crystallography and in string theory, scientists have found new applications for Ramanujan's formulae. His formulae are like a genetic code for digital-world technology. He failed many other subjects at the cost of his main interests in mathematics.

There is no academic training that can make you Ramanujan, because academic training is not aimed at evoking your natural skills. This is why I say that your certificates do not evoke what you are. If you make too much of an emphasis about your technical expertise, you will miss the chance of seeing what you are. It is a fact that every one of us has natural skill like Ramanujan. I see that as a fact, not as an opinion. When we put more of an emphasis on certificates, we ignore our natural skills.

Tiger Woods (Florida, USA, born 1975) is one of the most successful golfers of all time and he began to play golf at the age of two. At the age of eight, he first won the 'Optimist International Junior tournament'. According to his biography and various reports, my impression is that this boy expresses what is natural to him.

Vijay Pabbathi

> My understanding is that natural abilities are linked to a grand scheme of evolution in which we play a role.

Such a grand plan may be beyond the imagination of man but will benefit mankind. Our problem is that we keep arguing about ideas, words, and explanations without seeing the facts. You will need the nerve to go beyond the words and discover whether you have a unique skill like Tiger Woods.

Shakuntala Devi (Bangalore, India, 1939) demonstrated her natural skills of calculating numbers at the age of three. In 1980, she demonstrated the multiplication of two thirteen-digit numbers picked at random by the Computing Department of Imperial College, London, in twenty-eight seconds. My understanding is that everyone has a better mind than a computer. When the child is curious about something, he can bring something from the unknown. It is important for parents to recognise such natural qualities in children and nourish them further to evoke the innate abilities of children.

If we want to compare our children with other children and make them strive for the first mark in a group or a class, how can the child spends his psychological energy in a natural area of interest? What many parents are doing in the modern world is making a royal road for their children to escape from their natural abilities by making them earn a livelihood and respectability in society. By doing so we claim

Unknown Truth of Life

that we love them. Few children are like Shakuntala Devi and escape from such turmoil and get a chance to express their innate strengths.

Blaise Pascal (French mathematician and physicist, 1623–62) contributed to mathematics from the age of eleven or twelve. His abilities relating to natural and applied sciences were natural to him. He made important contributions to both mathematics and physics. It was noted in history that Descartes refused to believe that Pascal had accomplished such precocious work. How could a small boy who was not taught at academic schools solve major problems in mathematics?

In my understanding, Pascal had an early opportunity to express his natural abilities. We all have natural skills. We never bother to express them because there is a pressure in families and society for to earn a livelihood and reach one of the top positions. That is where we spend our time and energy, by permanently ignoring what we are. I am not suggesting that you can be Pascal. I am suggesting that you have something precious within you like Pascal had. Diversity is a fundamental property of Nature. Your skills could be so different that the world has never seen them before. How do you know unless you cancel your busy schedule and find out what you are?

S. P. Balasubrahmanyam (Andhra Pradesh, India, 1946) has sung more than 39,000 songs in more than five different Indian languages. During 1997, I had a chance to listen his songs in a live programme in Coventry, UK. He used to sing classical film songs with effortless ease. He is a truly gifted signer who has incredible vocal range and style. As he mentioned to me, during our meeting, he never had any formal training in singing.

In my understanding, simply learning a skill to fit social requirements cannot make a person outstanding. If the singer is more important than the song, then you will see only yourself struggling for accolades. If the song is more important than the singer, then you have a chance to disappear in meditation and will see nature's beauty in it.

Personal example: I never had formal teacher training. Many of my students regard me as one of the best teachers in both formal and informal feedback sessions. I never prepare what words or expressions I will use in my lectures. On many occasions, I disappear in silence whenever I am teaching. I lose track of time during my teaching. I remember myself in a classroom when students laugh or if there is a disturbance. I never tried to be the best teacher or the best presenter. I have the same energy and attention whether I teach one student or 100 students. The external appearance of teaching is linked to internal mediation; this activity gave me a new psychological birth and the chance to interact with other human beings in a different dimension. Based on what is happening to me whenever I teach, I realised that teaching is natural to me.

*   *   *

Reason excludes natural abilities

Adherence to logic does not necessarily generate true (natural) solutions. In order to access true solutions in any aspect of life, I prefer to use both logical and non-logical insights when required. Thus, there is a possibility of accessing natural (true) solutions.

Adherence to logic is adherence to the logical part of the mind that prevents the expression of natural abilities as opposed to intellectual abilities. Thus it is highly likely that the more educated you are, the less natural you become, unless you understand how logical thinking functions. Logical arguments also occupy the mind, which will create a totally unnatural life drama in which there is no chance to realise natural abilities.

Logic can be used as and when needed once a person discovers innate abilities as part of his expression of abilities. Logic can catalyse the natural abilities of individuals, but it cannot help to discover innate abilities.

For most people, it is extremely difficult to accept their natural abilities because accepting the natural state (or innate ability) appears to be absurd, based on intellectual thinking. When the intellect accepts the natural state, its function is reduced. If a person is expressing natural abilities, the function of intellectual affairs is marginal. Since accepting the natural state depends on the reduction of the importance of being intellectual, it is extremely difficult for individuals to accept their natural skills. On other hand, the intellect likes to make an effort to get training or to be efficient over time. It accepts those issues or plans in which it can play a part. If the effort is not involved in work, the intellect sees that this affair is insane. Thus the intellectual perception that does not accept natural abilities is not based on the validity of the natural abilities, but is truly based on the fact that intellect will be excluded as soon as the natural ability is accepted.

* * *

Please observe your children while you are spending time with them. Maintain a notebook to write your observations about them. Your observations should not be related to what you want them to be or what you like about them. The observations must be related to the things that they are doing without being told. What is that they do naturally? For example, if your baby is fixing a computer without using a user manual, that is a valuable observation. If a child is fixing something or doing something without prior expertise or guidance, that untrained skill has utmost value to the life of your child. Such observations must be listed to. If children are guided to follow their natural skills, as opposed what you want them to become, they will become very happy people. If you give little help in the direction that they are naturally propelled, they will contribute to the world in way that the world has never seen before.

Importantly, it is useful to make a note about the behavioural aspects of the child. You need to make a note about both good and bad behaviour. It is important that you should not be biased in making the observations and not projecting your thoughts about your child. If you write what you choose to write, your notes will harm your child. Write about what you see in them. You should make the observations of your child as if you are a headless chicken. If you use your head, your notes become a bunch of wish lists, which will harm your children.

* * *

Application

1. I will explore what I am and what my natural ability is. I understand that expression of my own nature leads me to find the meaningful life.

2. I will explore what I was good at as a child and see whether my childhood interests are related to my innate abilities that will bring a peaceful life.

3. I understand that my weaknesses are part of me for evolutionary reasons. I will explore whether my weaknesses are linked to my natural skills, rather than changing myself to hide the weaknesses.

4. I will deliberately deal with disappointments to explore whether my natural skills can be expressed while I am dealing with disappointing life affairs.

8. The Certainty of Life

Insights

When man actually observes the nature of a conflicting mentality (thinking process) that is trying desperately to solve the problems of life, then there is intelligence, which brings certainty in life. Man becomes spontaneously intelligent, not by seeking a method to solve the problems, but by identifying his own nature, which is unconsciously creating problems.

In a nutshell

Certainty of life appears when you do not conflict with what you are trying to accomplish.

Many of us are highly encouraged in society to reach a top position regardless of the field of our studies. Being an expert in a field is highly regarded among intellectuals who face tremendous social pressure to draw the highest salary or to earn respectability in society. Society provides a model, based on social applause and the expertise required. When we try to accomplish what fits in society, because our livelihood is entangled with social requirements, there is always fear in our actions. The fear in our actions engenders uncertainty in life.

There is always fear in our actions in the pursuit of achieving something that is appreciated by society. When man ignores his own nature and struggles to follow the model provided by society, he naturally can not find fulfilment and peace in his own actions. We are always encouraged to learn know-how or method so that we can accomplish everything that we want. As part of our life journey, we always find motivation regarding 'how to be lucky', 'how to earn millions of dollars', 'how to win friends', or 'how to attract everything we want'. There are so many methods available in society to knead the mind in a way that society expects you to live.

Alternatively, there is another model available with spiritual teachers who are expected to know about life better than us. As part of spirituality or religious teachings, many wise men (saints, Babhas, seers, prophets, philosophers, and saviours) begin to suggest 'how to live', and there is another model that may suggest an eight-fold path, spiritual secrets, and so forth. These systems prompt one to follow someone else's (like Buddha) nature as opposed to making us psychologically independent of systems. In the pursuit of accomplishing man's ambitions, the spiritual methods are invented and these methods appear to deliver peace, pleasure, and happiness. Man is poised to receive more of these methods because the amount of pleasure (or incentive) has become the measure.

Many people like to have a method of practice or a system of principles to practice so that they can have a set of guideposts though the journey of life. Man always invests time and energy in using methods or systems of practice, because method shows a starting point to begin the practice. There are many methods available in spiritual practices.

Examples of such systems are Buddhism, Christianity, Hinduism, and so forth. Adherents of each system exclude something that is valuable in other systems based on their attachment to their system of choice. Scientists also follow 'logic-based thinking', which is another system of rules, and they exclude everything that does not fit in with the logic. If the facts cannot be perceived using experimental evidence and measurable quantities, man tends to ignore them. That is one of the fundamental limitations of science. If man ignores certain facts based on his system of practice, does it matter whether he is scientific or spiritual? Is it possible for man to be psychologically free from the limitations of the system of his choice? Unless man is able to see the truth outside the scope of the system of his choice, can he consider anything that is dependable?

Millions of people entered into systems such as Buddhism or Hinduism. Only a few dozen enlightened masters came out of these systems. The success rate is fractional and negligible according to any standard that can be imagined, which means that it is not the system that is making people intelligent. None of your body organs care which system you follow. That is a fact. How does it matter to the beating heart or respiratory system, whether you worship Jesus, Krishna, or Buddha?

Whether we take the social model or spiritual model as opposed to living in our own live, the uncertainty remains, regardless of our cultural or national background. The questions remains: through what method does the life become certain? Whenever we seek for a solution, we unconsciously search for a method (know-how), which has to deliver the end result and accomplish progress in linear fashion. It is important to investigate whether we need a method at all to see the certainty of life? Is it possible to see the solution for our problems without spiritual or social systems? Is there anything that science or spirituality cannot solve? Let us begin to enquire.

*   *   *

As far as technological and scientific advancements are concerned, we are using the human mind. When we apply our thinking process to our own life, our minds function like an underdeveloped mind (the monkey mind). Let me explain why the mind behaves like a monkey's mind when we deal with life affairs. A few examples are given here:

1. We want to deal with life affairs intelligently and we want to accomplish progress in a linear fashion. As explained in chapter three, involving intellectual affairs in seeking progress in a linear fashion that makes the mind impermeable to the facts of life. Thus the mind that ignores the facts of life cannot be intelligent. In this process, the fear about the end results cannot be avoided. Thus, man wants to possess two mutually exclusive events (being intelligent and having continuous progress) that conflict with each other.

2. Man wants to be famous and also wishes to be creative individual. The mind that is constantly trying to be famous wastes tremendous psychological energy and it cannot be creative. For more description about this insight, please see chapter four. The creative mind will not be involved in petty affairs like becoming famous. Thus man appears to be in conflict with is own behaviour of being famous while he is desperate to generate the creative output.

3. Man wishes to achieve time-bounded results in order to achieve his goals and he also wants to discover his natural abilities. Discovering natural events requires appreciating the natural time-scale required to see natural process. If we are in a rush to gain certain

incentives, there is no possibility to discover innate ability. Thus man conflicts with his own behaviour. Discovering or expressing innate ability cannot be within the limitations of time-bounded events.

4. Man wants to accomplish serendipitous discovery while struggling to accomplish fixed goals. For a detailed description of this insight, please see chapter five. How can we accomplish unknown results (the serendipitous discovery) unless our goals are flexible? The mentality that appreciates the serendipitous discovery is the same mentality that struggles to achieve the fixed goals.

5. Many people want to be superior to other people in society. We want to be recognised with prizes and titles while we campaign to bringing about universal brotherhood. Externally man wants to be an enlightened individual while he preaches about equality or compassion. Man's physical outfit (dress code, gospel, symbols, and so forth) creates a psychological division among people, and there is no possibility of being equals as long as you think that your system of practice is superior compared with the systems of other individuals. How can the mind that is constantly seeking and accomplishing its superiority over other people bring equality? Are you not excluding the outcome of your choice by the nature of your practice? By calling yourself enlightened, how can a common man negate the psychological division between himself and others? As long as your actions simultaneously create

Unknown Truth of Life

social and psychological divisions, can you ever bring the outcome that you have been seeking?

6. There are numerous examples in society in which people follow teachers such as Buddha. Man wants to follow one of the great masters, based on a variety of reasons including the quest for enlightenment. How is enlightenment to come to man if he is psychologically dependent on his masters? Psychological dependency on his masters will exclude the outcome that he is looking for. If a man can not respect his own nature and if he depends on his masters for something that is not part of his own nature, can he live with peace? My emphasis is that 'being yourself and being Buddha' are mutually exclusive. (You can replace the word Buddha with another master. It does not matter which name we use in this example.) How can a man follow Buddha and be himself simultaneously? If he does not depend on his own nature, how he is going to attain the enlightenment? By negating what is naturally yours and following someone else's nature, is it possible for man to have meaningful life?

When you exclude your own nature in the pursuit of following Buddha, you conflict with your own nature. It is unlikely that you will express someone else's genetic code, even if you struggle for your whole life. By following Buddha, it is likely that you will neither become Buddha nor live in your own life. Buddha's nature is not part of your genetic code and therefore you will not become Buddha regardless of your struggle to do so. Furthermore, by preaching others' teachings that are not based on your own life experiences, you will create problems for yourself and also create problems for others. There is no need to take my word for this. Please investigate this for yourself. (Buddha himself attained enlightenment when he ignored all other teachings and followed himself, according to history.) Whoever the master you want to follow is, regardless of my insights that emphasise this, you will not attain favourable results by ignoring your own nature.

I am not debating about Buddha or his teachings. My discussion is related to the mentality that tries to accomplish enlightenment while following Buddha. It is the mind that seeks psychological security from following Buddha is the mind that is also trying to achieve ultimate fulfilment (or enlightenment), which will be excluded by its own behaviour. As long as your master is more important than your life and your own nature, your conflict with your own actions is inevitable. When you have a conflict with your own nature, life can never appear certain. The certainty that is felt in absence of psychological independence is not certainty at all.

The conflicting nature of our thinking (intellect) is built into everything we pursue. No spiritual or scientific concept can save man, unless he understands how our thinking process is actually excluding what we want to accomplish.

> It is not the spiritual method that makes the man intelligent. If you see the nature of the conflicting mentality that is desperate for a method or system of practice, you will stop creating problems for yourself and others.

It is important to understand that it is the mentality that is trying to seek answers within a system is the same mentality that is also creating the problems. It is entirely possible for anyone to be intelligent, not by solving problems within a system, but by actually seeing the conflicting behaviour of intellect (mentality). Once you see the real nature of your own mentality, does it matter what system it follows in solving problems? As I see it, it makes no difference whether you are spiritual or scientific as long your mentality is conflicting with you inwardly and outwardly.

You can solve problems once and for all only when you use your energy to see that 'the mind that is trying to solve the problems using systems is the mind that is creating the problems'. You can bring a hundred or more systems or methods, but the monkey (intellect) will behave the same way – it cannot be intelligent unless it realises the futility of its own behaviour. As long as you try to solve a problem with a method or system it seeks progress in a linear fashion and becomes unintelligent because its primary interest is to maintain what it is doing. It cannot get out of it once it goes inside the systems. As long as you are psychologically dependent on someone or something, your life cannot be certain.

In my understanding, these systems are like morphine; while the morphine is useful for relieving pain, the mind wants morphine again and again. Unless you have the ability to ignore the morphine after the pain is relieved, health cannot be restored. As long as the pain is relieved by the use of painkillers, relieving the pain appears to be truth. Thus, the personal requirement of meeting the psychological demand appears to be truth when you are part of a system.

The problem is that the pain keeps coming again and again. There is no end to this, unless we explore the root cause of the pain. All these systems are like painkillers, and they make us psychologically dependent on systems. Being satisfied with a psychological urge appears to be true to a man who has been following systems, because the experimenter (you) is part of the experiment (your own life). An experimenter who is conducting experiments ignores the physiological limitations of his cognitive abilities. Instead, what he is allowed to see appears to be true to him without addressing the limits of his perceptions.

Unless you are aware of the limitations, strengths, and weakness of the system of your choice, you will be permanently locked into that system. It is nobody's fault. It happens unconsciously because the mind wants something that functions in a linear fashion in whatever it pursues – and it is not inclined to change the way it functions. A set of rules or a system is like a set of tools – if you do not understand the limits of the tools, you may assume that 'using the tool is the truth'.

What is happening to man is that man begins with a system because following a system is an easier way to deal with intellectual affairs as opposed to having psychological independence. Then he gets locked into the system because following a system appears to be true – and therefore he is led away from the journey he began when he decided to follow the system. When following a system, the mind enjoys the status quo. Can the functional limitations of being in the status quo deliver the truth?

The political atmosphere in any system (including religious and scientific ones) cannot be avoided. For example, scientists often become locked into a system of logical thinking. If I say use logic as and when needed, it appears absurd to the scientific community. In reality, unless a scientist goes beyond logic, there is no way that he will be useful to science. When logic becomes too important, man gives less importance to life and the petty fights among people cannot be solved. The growth of consciousness becomes stunted as long as man does not see the limits of the system in which he is invested.

*　　*　　*

Let us consider the analogy that 'growing a beard requires shaving blades'. As long as a beard is growing, man needs shaving blades. Therefore, the market for shaving blades will never perish because man's beard grows incessantly. There is a demand and a supply. If man does not want shaving blades, these companies that make shaving blades disappear automatically. Similar to this analogy, as long as you breed problems and holy men (seers, sages, monks, sanyasins, bhabas, and bhagavans) appear, these men provide various spiritual methods that will temporarily satisfy your demands. The appearance of holy men in the market place is an indicator that our life problems have not been solved yet. None of the methods will eradicate our problems because we continuously breed the problems with our conflicting nature.

> As long as man wants to accomplish progress in a linear fashion, there is a need for a spiritual teacher or psychologist to solve his problems.

As long as man wants to accomplish progress in a linear fashion, there is a lucrative market for spirituality. This is because man breeds problems inescapably. If you do not create problems through your way of living, you will laugh at the entire spiritual heritage and associated methods. By seeking the spiritual methods, you are essentially seeking something to alleviate your pain, which will reoccur again and again. You can not root out the pain unless you see what causing the pain.

Unknown Truth of Life

Whether you want spiritual methods to solve your problems is your decision. However, if you begin to see the mentality that is seeking to be superior to others in the society, you will not need spiritual methods. Destroying temples or churches, engaging in holy wars, or arguing about 'which system is best' will not make you intelligent. Maturity and psychological independence comes to you once you understand that your approaches to life are excluding what you are looking for. Why do you need a holy man to understand this fact?

You will constantly receive new methods or systems to meet with your psychological demands, similar to the analogy of being offered a wide range of shaving blades as long as man's beard is growing. What you have been offered is to satisfy your urge and give you hope to maintain your status quo. If you are not provided with hope, you will not go to holy men. Therefore, the seekers and masters condition each other and serve each other rather than addressing the fundamental problem. If any teacher addresses the fundamental problem, as opposed to providing hope to satisfy psychological urge, you will not listen, because having psychological satisfaction is your measure. It is your decision whether you want to root out the basic problem in your thinking permanently. I have no urge to change anyone.

You will need a holy man if you create problems and seek solutions simultaneously. If not a holy man, you may seek help from a psychologist, as long as you do not like what is natural to you. If you do not tolerate what is a natural situation or process, you will need someone's help.

> If you want continuous profits, continuous pleasure, continuous peace, continuous happiness, continuous health, and continuous love from your partner, then you will need a holy man or psychologist – because anything that is continuous is bounded to exclude from nature.

> It is the nature of man's thinking process that it creates the problems for which he simultaneously seeks solutions.

When you seek help from a spiritual teacher or a psychologist, what is that you are looking for? Have you ever asked yourself 'what is the answer I am looking for?' Do you want to retain everything in a continuous fashion, and therefore you are seeking help (or method) that sustains your continuity? Whether we like it or not, it is a fact that nothing can be retained continuously in the universe. Whatever the help you may seek, however holy or noble the help may appear, all your solutions are false because sooner or later nature retains its discontinuity.

Unknown Truth of Life

If you accept that life functions in a non-linear fashion like everything in nature, you will laugh at all those spiritual methods. As long as you wish to be famous and superior to others, your problems are inescapable – and therefore there is a need for a spiritual or religious method. If you are prepared to be anonymous, you will not seek a spiritual guru and you will not look for someone to satisfy your psychological demands. If your goals are fixed and you are desperate to achieve whatever you want, then you will have a tremendous need for a spiritual master who can alleviate your neurotic attitude. If your goals are flexible, and if you are keen to find what is natural to you, you will not even think about enlightened masters. If you express your natural abilities as way of your life, you will laugh at the whole concept of enlightenment.

> If you encourage your children to
> be psychologically independent of
> spiritual/ religious systems, and
> dependent on their own nature,
> you can let them live peaceful lives
> regardless of the material wealth you
> may provide.

If you force your children to earn the prize, based on social applause or pressure, you will ultimately need

Bhagavans (seers) to help your children. The emphasis is not on the sages or religious systems; the emphasis is on your mentality that is seeking prize.

> Whenever there is a prize, there is competition - which excludes brotherhood among people and engenders animosity

There is a constant encouragement in society to find a job that is highly respectable, as opposed to following your own path in life. The same society will provide you with a wide range of spiritual methods to pacify your neurotic behaviour, which are inherent in the pursuit of earning a highly respectable position. We are unconsciously breeding problems and consciously seeking new solutions. We think we are becoming intelligent by asking questions like: how do we solve humanity's problems?

> You will be an intelligent person, not when you solve the problem, but when you discover that it is your 'mentality that is creating the problem'.

As long as you have pain, someone else will always sell painkillers in the market place. It is a futile effort to fight with the companies who sell painkillers. Similarly, there are always holy men who will bring new methods to satisfy peoples' need for belief systems. Their appearance is an indicator that more and more people are dealing the life unintelligently. It is important to understand that there is no need to ridicule any saint or sage who is offering services to meet your psychological satisfaction.

The seers will automatically disappear if your way of life is not creating problems to your life. The disappearance of methods, religious systems, or people who preach 'how to live' can be regarded as benchmark for the development of a society. If we know how to live without creating fear in our actions, and if we are handling our lives intelligently, we will not see any religious or spiritual system in the market place.

I wish to emphasise that as long as your life is more important than any system, you will be able to live your own life and only use these systems if they are needed. If a system becomes more important than your life, this system will use you and cripple your understanding of life.

In summary, it is possible to deal the life affairs with certainty if the conflicting ways of the thinking processes are understood. Such intelligence does not come by following a method or holy men, and it is not the method or system that makes man intelligent. As long as you are busy using the system or method, your understanding is marginal and you cannot avoid the problems of life.

* * *

Applications

1. I realized that 'life is more important than any religious system or spiritual master'. Therefore, I will give priority to life over spiritual methods or religious systems.

2. I will explore what brings certainty to my life. As part of my investigation, I will use any scientific or spiritual insight as and when it is required rather than being an adherent of one of these systems.

3. I will investigate whether there are any conflicting patterns within my own behavior that hinder my progress. Instead of searching for spiritual methods to solve life's problems, I will observe my mentality that is struggling to solve the problems.

9. The Absolute Truth

Insights

Absolute truth and psychological security are mutually exclusive and cannot live together in the same mind. When man has clarity that 'seeking hope' or fulfilling 'psychological demands' is not absolute truth, there will be a psychological mutation that opens a new door in consciousness.

The activity of worshipping is an intellectual affair. If man stops finding the 'absolute truth' through intellectual affairs such as worshipping, he will have the possibility of realising that worshipper and worshipped are the same. Otherwise, the distance between the worshipper and worshipped remains the same as long there is worship.

In a nutshell

If you understand 'the state of mind' that is trying to worship, you will understand the worshiped.

Man is always keen to find the unknown or absolute truth, which can also be referred to as God. When I use the word God, I am not talking about the descriptor or the word. My discussion is about the described (the higher reality of existence). Many of us know that the descriptor (the word) is not the described (the absolute truth).

How do we understand or perceive absolute truth? Can we find the truth by going to churches, temples, or monasteries? Can we find the truth by repeating words or mantras or using cross-legged postures? Can we find the absolute truth by having repeated meetings with gentlemen who might have long beards, shaven heads, or orange robes? Through what technique or faculty can we approach the truth?

* * *

If you are a believer in god, you may suggest that god is a fact. If god is a fact for you, you have to know how to find the facts in the search. Explanations, ideas, or thoughts about god will lead nowhere because the ideas exclude the facts, as previously mentioned. Without having the ability to find facts from life affairs, there is no possibility of discovering the reality of existence (which can also be referred as 'Absolute Truth' or God).

This is important because man overestimates the strength of ideas and intellectual capabilities, because ideas have been useful to science and technology. Therefore man uses ideas to find God (The Truth). If god is regarded as

Unknown Truth of Life

fact, ideas that are aimed at showing the existence of god become futile. All your gospels, mantras, justifications, and efforts, such as showing that the saviour can walk on water, show that you are trying to meet the demands of your own psychological pressure as opposed to discovering the facts.

Merely arguing about the existence of god, or justifying the existence of god, are futile efforts. Thoughts cannot discover the unknown (God). Man's way of approaching the absolute truth is through religions, gospels, symbols, scriptures, and so forth.

The idea that 'God does not exist' is a fact to atheists. If you believe that god does not exist, then you need to show that as a fact. To see something as fact, you need to find out what enables man to see the facts as they are. That means that merely arguing, showing evidence, or justification leads you astray. All your ideas, theories, and hypotheses that are attempting to show that *'God does not exist'* are futile. Once you perceive the fact, regardless of the nature of that fact, you will understand the futility of your debates. This is primarily because the mind learns how to see the facts and becomes intelligent in dealing with your issues and concerns intelligently. You will automatically understand that the fact you have seen does not need to be supported when you really perceive the fact. Such perception is not based on intellectual justifications.

Both theists and atheists need to know how to discover the facts, either to prove or disprove the existence of god. You need to know the art of finding facts whether you are working in science or spirituality. Finding facts is important to everybody and it is not relevant to fields or faculty. Otherwise, we merely argue with other people and waste our time in showing evidence and justifications. The idea has a limitation and the fact does not have such limitations because the facts are eternal and they exist whether man exists or not.

When two people argue about god, it is easy to see that both people argue about the descriptor (word). This is because one explanation can be intellectually debated using another set of words or dogmas. Let us assume a simple example: that the rotation of the earth is a fact. Do you think that the rotation of the earth requires you to support this as a fact? Does it matter whether you support it or not? Can man change the rotation of the earth by attracting a number of supporters to this belief? When you see something as a fact, as factual as the rotation of the earth, where is the need to have a number of supporters or arguments?

When an observer really (not verbally or intellectually) discovers the absolute truth, there is a side effect along with the true observation to the observer. That is: the observer understands the futility of the intellect that is trying to project the facts as it wants to see them. That side effect, which can be acquired with the ability to see the facts as they are, makes the mind intelligent. I am not talking about the intelligence with which you can send a rocket into space. I am talking about the intelligence that sees the futility of the intellect. When you see the futile and petty ways of intellect, you cannot behave stupidly.

Unknown Truth of Life

When you really understand what has been described, not through the intellectual faculties, but in reality, you will have nothing to argue about. If you are arguing about the existence or non-existence of god, your concerns are related to the descriptor. When you do not have the ability to feel the described, then you will worry about your descriptions, evidences, mantras, and gospels.

It appears to me that most people repeat the same words that have been mentioned in the ancient scriptures such as the Bible or Bhagavat Gita. If someone says your sacred scripture is useless, you will become angry because you did not understand what is exactly written and you never verified those statements using your own life experiences.

You might have used the sayings of Krishna to claim that India is great. Your claim is related to an accolade to your country, or pride. If you really understand Krishan, you will never argue about Krishna. Since your adherence is related to the descriptor or words, there is every possibility that the intellect will become angry because it does not want to be seen as stupid. When you truly understand the Gita and the meaning behind what is mentioned, perhaps you will laugh at a person who does not care about the Gita.

The reality of life consists of a mixture of pleasures and sorrows. The mind doesn't want the mixture; the mind starts separating the pain from the pleasure, good luck from bad luck, success from failure, and in doing so, fear, confusion, and uncertainty arise. To avoid uncertainty, man needs to know the art of discovering the facts. If you are trying to do any activity other than finding the facts, your actions represent meeting the demands of your psychological insecurity.

Thoughts cannot give any clues about the existence of god. The question of whether god exists is outside the scope of this book.

> All the thoughts that are put together, however sacred the thoughts may be, serve to provide hopes and meet psychological insecurity. Intellectual approaches to understanding the sacred scriptures will deliver the results that you are looking for and not the truth.

In my understanding, as long as the mind is entangled in profit-oriented thinking or certain incentives, there is no possibility that it will see certain facts beyond the psychological urge for incentives. Man's mentality has an element of self-interest built into it that excludes the facts. It is not the self-interest that creates the problem. The serious problem arises when man wants to retain self-interest and also wants to find the truth, which is the basis for conflicting interest. When the self-interest ends, truth appears. Having awareness that these qualities are mutually exclusive, you cannot waste time by trying to accomplish them simultaneously. This is your decision.

The quality of mind that is able to see the truth does not even think about self-interest. In such a pursuit of combining self-interest with the truth, man makes an investment in all sorts of gods that are poised to satisfy his demands. If you are able to see the futility of man's efforts and man's conflicting interests in the pursuit of discovering the higher reality, then you cannot be childish.

I am not advocating that you should not have self-interest. My emphasis is on revealing that you cannot discover the absolute truth as long as there is self-interest. That is the cost of discovering the higher reality (God). I do not want you to waste your time by running around in the pursuit of discovering the absolute truth while you wish to maintain all of your personal interests. This is your choice. I have no inclination to push you either way.

Paradox of hope

Hope is not a fact. Whenever there is a psychological insecurity, man seeks hope. Hopes give psychological satisfaction whereas the facts make the mind intelligent.

It does not matter which god you worship or which religion or doctrine you follow. This is because most religions provide hope and meet the psychological demands of man. What is happening to man when he goes to religious services? Having hope or meeting psychological demands is seen as truth – which is a false perception.

Hope maintains the need to achieve progress in a linear fashion. The very process of search or seeking something excludes you from your natural state. Thus hope, while we all want to have it, excludes man from truth. By being hopeful, man approaches whatever he wants intellectually. That intellectual affair, which helps you in science and the advancement of technology, will not help you in spiritual faculty.

The facts exist beyond perceptions that are subjected to pain and pleasures. If your measure is based on amounts of pleasure, your thinking wanders in business activities that are fundamentally incentive or profit-based. However, in the spiritual field, if pleasure is going to be your measure, your delusions are unavoidable in the pursuit of discovering the absolute truth.

You may gain your profits if you expand the pleasure element and provide the activities that generate pleasure to your customers. If you are trying to use the same logic in serving people in spiritual world, you will delude yourself and others. This is your decision. My emphasis is about the mentality that handles the sacred scriptures; it is not about the contents of the scriptures.

Psychological comforts make you impermeable to the truth, although they are valued in society. For example, psychological comforts that are based on worship or religious activity in sacred places are highly valued in different cultures. If you are serious about finding the absolute truth, your inquiry needs to be go beyond psychological comforts. Otherwise, it is a waste of your time and will delude you. It is fundamental to understand that what society appreciates is not necessarily the truth.

Almost all religions give hope and provide psychological security, thus the mind forgets about finding the facts – the psychological situations do not make the mind intelligent. I am not saying that one should not try to find hope. My emphasis is that facts exist beyond meeting the psychological demand for hope. If you are serious about finding the facts, then you need to have a keen eye to see the reality of existence beyond psychological demands.

*   *   *

Worshipping a scripture?

It is common knowledge that each of the sacred scriptures contain many useful insights or suggestions that can be used for a way of living. My concern is that what makes the man understand those insights suggested in sacred scriptures. It is my impression that many people do not apply the suggested teachings in their individual life circumstances. I have personally tested some of the concepts presented in the scriptures of Taoism, Buddhism, Christianity, and Hinduism. When I really applied those concepts, without having any adherence or reverence to any of these isms, then all the intellectual debates about those teachings became meaningless. What I felt was that all of those intellectual debates have a role to a man who never verifies these concepts in individual life situations. When you have not verified the insights presented in the scriptures, then you have plenty to argue about.

When I verified those concepts, as mentioned above, my priority was to use the concept if it helps my life (or throw away the insights that were not useful), regardless who suggested those concepts. I felt that I would have not understood the insights presented by various masters if I were to merely adhere to one of those systems, or if I was trying to involve myself in worship as opposed to personally validating teachings in my own life circumstances. It does not matter whether you worship intellect, ideas, scriptures, or Buddhas. The nature of worship creates the same psychological effect in the human mind.

Based on my understanding, the activity of worship does not help man to achieve absolute understanding about scriptures or masters. You may repeat the words that you memorise and preach the same words from these scriptures; however, you will lose an important skill that perceives the truth unconsciously as part of the worshiping process.

> A doctrine, however sacred, cannot
> be more important than life
> — because the truth exists in life and
> is integral to living, unlike a dead
> scripture.

Unknown Truth of Life

When man gives more importance to a scripture, he attributes importance to his intellectual affairs and what he calls is sacred becomes detrimental to the life. In history, many millions of people were massacred in many parts of the world in the name of the sacred scriptures and religions. When life becomes less important than a scripture, saviour, or religion, man inevitably destroys himself and others.

People who use scriptures or religions to inform their daily living may not agree with me, based on the fact that they have conflict of interest with their business activities as opposed to the truth of the situation. This is why a view from a holy man is irrelevant to my analysis, based on the simple reason that there is a conflict of interest based on what holy man sees as an intensive.

Giving importance to doctrines is an intellectual affair that functions in the same way whether you sit in a boardroom or a monastery.

> If the doctrine becomes more important than life, man lives with dead consciousness, and he destroys the society in the name of spiritual heritage.

On other hand, if helping your life is your priority and if you have the nerve to drop all of the sacred scriptures at the cost of helping life, then you will help yourself and others. This is your decision. It is not my focus to change anyone.

* * *

Worshipping a teacher?

Man's way of approaching the truth is worshipping the saviour or teacher and unconsciously losing the truth of the teachings. When a teacher becomes important in our minds, the truth of his teachings is unconsciously ignored. When a painter is important, the truth of the painting is ignored.

> The only way to understand the truth of the teachings is to treat the teachers as your equal (as a friend) and verity the teachings in real life situations. Only then, the mind will be relieved of its intrinsic barriers and see the truth of the teachings.

Worshipping the teachers is an escape mechanism of the mind from true understanding. The nature of worship within the human psychological space remains the same, regardless of culture, religion, or nationality. As I see it, man escapes from understanding the reality of existence as long as the worship is continued.

Worshipping a saviour may give 'feel-good' psychological perceptions. However, the nature of worship within the human mind makes you escape from having a complete understanding about the saviour and his teachings. In other words, man can understand Buddha completely when he stops worshipping him because the process of worship does not allow man to understand the worshipped. That means that a Buddhist can have an absolute understanding about the Buddha's teachings when he stops worshipping him and treats the Buddha as friend. This is not a debate about Buddha or his teachings. My discussion is about man's perceptions.

All those people walking around with shaven heads and orange robes may chant mantras and may have the expertise to talk about the philosophy of Buddha, but when they actually understand the original nature of 'Buddha as it is', perhaps they will laugh at the whole process of worship.

A Buddhist cannot be a Buddha as long as one is greater than another. If one is greater than the other, there is a division, which creates a psychological barrier. Division sanctions fear, which makes you stupid. When the mind is already stupid, what it calls a deep respect becomes fear-driven worship.

The idea of attaining Buddha-hood is an intellectual affair. 'Becoming', 'attaining', and 'accomplishing' are intellectual concepts. When perception becomes part of intellectual affairs, man has a tendency to design symbols, trademarks, and dress code. When you truly want to understand Buddha, do you need to be a Buddhist? What I am saying is also applicable to all other religions in general. I am taking the example of a Buddhist to explain my analysis.

External worship creates an unconscious psychological barrier that prevents the growth of consciousness and makes an easy escape from the facts. When the mind is occupied in doing rituals, the mind simultaneously escapes from the state of mind that is required to understand and verify concepts. This is because we do not doubt the master who has presented the concept. If you do not doubt the master and do not have the nerve to brush aside everything that you have learned from the scriptures at the cost of your life, your understanding is limited. This is why it appears to me that a non-Buddhist has a better chance of understanding Buddha than people who spend their lives in monasteries. A non-Christian has a better chance of understanding Jesus than people who regularly go to churches. It is not the fault of the adherents. What I am saying is related to how our mind functions.

If you truly want to understand one of those teachers like Jesus, Krishna, or Buddha, begin with one teacher without worshipping him and test the concept he teaches, and then see what happens. If you go that far, you will not only understand your teacher, you will also understand the mentality of your teacher. Unless you grow to the level at which you understand your teacher's mentality, your understanding is limited.

If someone else says Jesus is stupid, you will be angry and be prepared to kill the person who says so. Have you ever applied Jesus' teachings in your own life to test the truth of what he said? What you know is probably the descriptor – not the described. Therefore, you tend to be angry when someone ridicules your descriptor. Adherence to the descriptors is again an intellectual affair that requires verbal garbage.

So when you say that you are worshipping Jesus or Buddha, what you are worshipping is your descriptors and your intellectual affairs. Therefore, you may not agree with the insights I am presenting. If you drop your worshipping nature, you will not be doing anything related to the described or higher reality.

The 'state of mind' that is trying to worship

One has to understand 'the state of mind' of worship. If you have the ability to walk on water, will you care whether someone else has the same? If you have the ability to turn water into wine, will you care whether someone else who has the same ability? It is basically the state of mind that if one cannot become something, in the pursuit of trying to become that thing, one tries to worship what one cannot be.

Whether you are spiritual or intellectual really does not matter. As long as you worship something, you will not understand the state of mind that is desperate to worship. If you have a chance to understand the state of mind that is desperately worshiping, you will encounter the worshiped. The point is that you will need to understand the limits of human perceptions in order to understand the state of mind that is seeking to worship.

Worshipping is an intellectual affair. Discovering the absolute truth is not an intellectual affair. The intellect that has created anxiety through activities seeking for linear progress or permanency has also created intellectual affairs to satisfy psychological demands. Unless man sees that satisfying personal demands is not the means to find the truth, there will not be any growth in his consciousness.

> Rituals that are part of worship give a psychological perception that 'something of higher value' is going on, and that therefore they must be right. In fact, everything related to rituals creates psychological satisfaction, which isolates man from truth.

A man who cannot see the facts as they are desperately depends on such psychological satisfaction because such satisfaction gives a perception that a higher order is being followed.

The feel-good atmosphere attained through rituals is an escape mechanism of the intellect to avoid finding facts. Such an atmosphere projects artificial meaning, which leads the believer to destroy humanity in the name of religious separations and holy wars. If man is able to find the facts as they are, then he spontaneously ignores all rituals and worships forthwith. In other words, the disappearance of religions and worship are the benchmarks to note the growth of man's consciousness, the development of his society, and civilisation in general.

*   *   *

Can science help find 'absolute truth'?

Science needs experimental evidence, which has to be obtained from an experiment in which the scientist has to be isolated from an experiment. If you are part of an experiment from which an observation is made, the observation is not trustworthy. The experimenter should not be part of an experiment if a valid observation has to be made. To discover the absolute truth, the observer's mind has to be in an isolated system other than himself – which makes it impossible for man to conduct such an experiment. This is the fundamental limit of science that tries to find the evidence for the existence of absolute truth or ultimate reality. The very understanding of the fact that science or logic-based thinking is the wrong tool to discover the higher reality itself is a major realisation, which does not come to you as long as you worship science.

Science requires measurement, whereas the absolute truth is regarded as immeasurable in many cultures. Science requires these measurements with respect to time, whereas the unknowable (The Absolute Truth) is regarded as timeless intelligence. How can we apply the time-based measurements on timeless intelligence?

Clarity about the limits of the science and logic-based thinking comes only when man understands the limits of his perceptions.

> If you are using science or logic based thinking to discover the absolute truth, then your efforts are like *'drinking water with a fork'*. That means that you are using a device that does not have a functional capability to discover the absolute truth.

As long as you worship science, you will not use science efficiently. Therefore it is extremely difficult for intellectuals to address their own limitations because they are adherent to science. When you understand the limitations of science, and when you do not use the tools for that which they are not applicable, you become an intelligent individual because you will not waste your time and energy on futile efforts.

If you are trying to fix a machine, then techniques and ideas will do wonders for you. Unfortunately, you cannot use the same kind of thinking that you apply to machines

Unknown Truth of Life

to discover the absolute truth. This is because when you are working with a machine, you are not part of the machine – and therefore the science can do wonders for you. Ideas or thoughts cannot influence the function of the same mind that is part of an investigation. You may be capable of launching a space shuttle and discovering new methods of transportation using your ideas. All those ideas that you apply externally will not lead you to discover the absolute truth, however.

The above-described understanding is based on observing the ways of Nature's Intelligence – which tells us that energy becomes dysfunctional at its source. For example, our eyes are useful to see many things. The eyes are not designed to see themselves. That is the functional limitation of the eyes. Similarly, you can use your fingers for many purposes, but the finger cannot be applied to itself. These examples are pointed out to stimulate understanding, and are not mentioned to justify the insight.

Accepting the limitations of science and understanding where science becomes useless does not mean that we are supporting holy men or theologies. What it means to me is that: scientists cannot be in the pursuit of debates about validating the existence of absolute truth.

> A scientist who tries to prove or disprove about the existence of God does not know the limitations of science. Such pursuits, however

scientific they may appear, they finally limit the cognitive abilities of man.

*   *   *

Applications

1. I will not enter into a debate about the 'existence of God' because I understand that all such debates are intellectual affairs that have no relation to the absolute truth.

2. I will deal with the facts of my life instead of seeking hope through rituals or religious activities.

3. I will investigate 'why am I psychologically depending on God?' and explore further to understand the state of mind that is craving for a higher reality.

*   *   *

10. Summary

When facing a problem in life, most people try to fix the problem to serve their psychological urge for security. What is more important than fixing a problem is seeing the roots of the problem and seeing the interconnectedness of the problem to various life events. This will helps us to understand a new dimension of life. If you are busy achieving progress according to your intellectual projections, you will not have a chance to observe the nature of the problem.

Understating the wholeness of life helps man to see both the successes and failures in life together, and to understand life in a new dimension. Such understanding prevents the waste of psychological energy by mere reactions to one's disappointments and focus on the successful areas of life.

As long as goals are fixed, life becomes compromised. The benediction begins when the goals are dynamically flexible and are less important than life. If goals are dynamically changing according to your own observations, you can transcend fear about the outcome. Thus the meaningful life appears as a shadow if the goals are flexible.

When man is absorbed in his accomplishments and ambitions, he finds no time to recognise the quality of life. A lack of time to understand life is a means of escape. When the mind is handling time-bounded pressures, it is impossible for it to have clarity about life. If the mind dissolves time-consciousness, it will have access to creative energy that does not come from intellect.

The goal of being respected in society will naturally sabotage your life and lives of your dependents. You will not live with your own life as long as you run around trying to be respected. The urge to be respected or to win a prize cannot be avoided unless you express your natural skills and involve yourself in generating creative output.

Society appreciates a number of both useful and useless actions. In fact, whatever is acclaimed by society is suspect and should be thoroughly verified in order to explore the roots of such applause. Otherwise, the mind will perceive whatever is acclaimed as the truth.

Understanding life happens when you understand that intellect is not everything and that man needs to go beyond the use of intellect. The intellect tries to deal with fragments of life affairs so that it can make an effort to achieve specific end results and it gives the perception that everything is fine if the targeted goal is achieved. These perceptions are right as long as the intellect is applied externally to fix machines. However, when life affairs are concerned, man needs perception of facts in order to lead life according to the facts.

Life becomes meaningful as long as your life is more important than your ideas and requirements.

If you are searching for an opportunity to prove or accomplish something with the pretext of finding meaning, please be aware of the psychological state that is looking for the meaning. The meaning of life will be clear only when you understand the state of mind that is looking for meaning. It is the nature of intellect that makes man to search for meaning, after the basic requirements of life are satisfied. Logical thinking that is extremely useful for survival will become a destructive instrument once the basic requirements of life are satisfied. This understanding requires personal exploration, as opposed to intellectual appreciation. If man is able to go beyond logical thinking, based on his own experience, clarity will appear like blooming flowers.

'What you are' and 'what is natural to you' makes you a creative individual who is not simply another copy in the world. Unless you express your creativity, you will end up destroying yourself and other people in the name of social divisions. When you really see the creative output from yourself, you will understand that you are part of this world and that you are the part of Nature's intelligence.

When a person knows his natural abilities and has flexible goals that he uses to see the facts in life situations, he will have a better chance of accessing the best possible opportunities in life. If a person expresses his natural abilities, his mind has very little to do. Regardless of the nature of one's innate abilities, one will lose track of time and unconsciously make the mind intelligent. If you go that far, your mind will stop searching for the meaning in life.

Seeing the natural solution in each event is far more important than struggling to achieve what one should become. What one should become makes one dull and moulds one's entire nature according to what society expects one to become.

THE END

Printed in the United Kingdom by
Lightning Source UK Ltd., Milton Keynes
137434UK00001B/304-420/P